redeeming CONFLICT

"Ann Garrido's *Redeeming Conflict* is a must for anyone engaged in pastoral ministry! It is an easy-to-read guide for understanding and even appreciating conflict as a practical way to move forward in relationships between persons and groups. The stories of saints and greats, known and unknown, are particularly interesting and insightful. Garrido's style is breezy and light, informed and rigorous. This book has the potential to make a great difference in how we, as persons and church, communicate, dialogue, and resolve problems."

Sr. Rose Pacatte, F.S.P.
Director of the Pauline Center for Media Studies

"In ministry contexts, where we find training in conflict styles, strategies, skills, and techniques, we are once again indebted to Ann Garrido for leading us through an enlightening theological reflection on our common human experience. Her exploration of discord leaves us with a solid grounding in our faith and inspiring guides from our robust tradition. Thank you, Ann, for helping us see the task of redeeming conflict as a lifelong calling to enter more deeply into the very heart of God."

David Lichter
Executive Director
National Association of Catholic Chaplains

"Every person in a leadership position—indeed anyone who is employed—should first be *required* to review this book. Dr. Garrido takes us on a journey of self-reflection through her questions at the end and throughout each chapter, which, if we are honest with ourselves, has the ability to transform the world's thinking."

Janice Edwards-Armstrong
Director of Leadership Education
Association of Theological Schools

"Ann Garrido's book *Redeeming Administration* was a hit with the principals in the Archdiocese of Los Angeles and taught us all that the 'ministry is in the interruption.' Now, with *Redeeming Conflict*, she teaches us that conflict is the mechanism whereby God 'matures creation.' While conflict is inevitable in both our work and personal lives, Garrido paints a wonderful picture of how we can effectively listen, navigate tensions, and live in communion with fellow travelers on this journey in faith."

Kevin Baxter
Senior Director and Superintendent of Schools
Archdiocese of Los Angeles

"An extremely readable and entirely useful guide to the inevitable conflict we all face every day. We can't wait to share Garrido's wise counsel with our entire parish team. You should share it with your team, too."

Rev. Michael White and Tom Corcoran
Authors of *Rebuilt*

"Ann Garrido shares great insight into leading God's people and facing conflict. She helps us become more self-aware and fosters pastoral sensitivity for those unavoidable times when we encounter discord and tension."

Most Rev. Gregory M. Aymond
Archbishop of New Orleans

redeeming CONFLICT

12 Habits for Christian Leaders

Ann M. Garrido

AVE MARIA PRESS AVE Notre Dame, Indiana

Founded in 1865, Ave Maria Press is a ministry of the United States Province of Holy Cross.

www.avemariapress.com

Paperback: ISBN-13 978-1-59471-613-3

E-book: ISBN-13 978-1-59471-614-0

Cover image © Thinkstock.com.

Cover and text design by Kristen Hornyak Bonelli.

Printed and bound in the United States of America.

Library of Congress Cataloging-in-Publication Data
Names: Garrido, Ann, 1969- author.
Title: Redeeming conflict : 12 habits for Christian leaders / Ann M. Garrido.
Description: Notre Dame : Ave Maria Press, 2016. | Includes bibliographical
  references.
Identifiers: LCCN 2015039194| ISBN 9781594716133 (pbk.) | ISBN 9781594716140
  (e-book)
Subjects: LCSH: Conflict management--Religious aspects--Christianity.
|
  Interpersonal relations--Religious aspects--Christianity.
Classification: LCC BV4597.53.C58 G37 2016 | DDC 253--dc23
LC record available at http://lccn.loc.gov/2015039194

This book is dedicated to

The Truth Circle

—Dominic, Eric, Scott,

Celeste, Dominic, and Sheila—

whose feisty friendship

launched this journey.

We must love them both,
those whose opinions we share
and those whose opinions we reject.
For both have labored in the search for truth
and both have helped us in the finding of it.

—Thomas Aquinas

Contents

Foreword

It is a cold morning in the north of England. I am struggling to write the eulogy for one of my closest friends. Two weeks earlier she had hugged me tight and said, "I'm afraid I won't see you again."

"Of course you will," I reassured. "I'll be back in two weeks. And the doctors say you have a month or two."

She didn't.

Jo was my friend and my sister-in-law. I gathered with family preparing for the funeral and wrestled with all the things we confront when we lose those we love. How would we make do without her? Where were we to find comfort, and how ought we comfort the daughters Jo left behind—aged only seven and three? I wrestled with the usual existential questions that profound loss brings: Why are we here on this earth? What do we accomplish? Does it matter?

On that rainy afternoon an e-mail quietly appeared—a brief note from a theologian in St. Louis. She had read the book I wrote with two colleagues at the Harvard Negotiation Project, *Difficult Conversations*. She was interested in learning more about how one might use it to better handle disagreement and conflict within church communities. As a faculty member at a Catholic theology school forming both seminarians and lay leaders for ministries around the world, Ann

Garrido had already started using *Difficult Conversations* to teach her students skills for handling tough conversations. But, she explained, she felt this wasn't enough.

"If we're serious about teaching people how to handle conflict constructively—with grace and discernment, curiosity and skill—it seems to me we need to be modeling how to do that as faculty and staff," Ann wrote. As a teacher of preaching, Ann thought they needed to be practicing what they were in fact preaching. Could I help?

I leapt at the invitation, partly because Ann's description of the ways conflict is handled—or mishandled—in Christian communities resonated with my own experience. As Christians we're not supposed to be having conflicts, or so it seemed in the strong Protestant church where I grew up in Lincoln, Nebraska. In my young mind's eye, Christians should be ever-giving and ever-forgiving, smiling as we turn the other cheek to those who persecute us with their sloppy preparation for Sunday school or forgotten promises to bring the potato salad. I didn't know a lot about Catholic seminary (we soon discovered that I couldn't spell "Eucharist." "We just call it the 'host,'" I replied, defensively), but I did recognize the ways that daily frustrations large and small can eat away at fellowship and community. I also knew that how we handle our hurt and disappointment often pulls us toward our least Christ-like selves.

I had been teaching negotiation, conflict resolution, and how to have "difficult conversations" for more than fifteen years at Harvard Law School and for both corporate and non-profit clients through our firm, Triad Consulting. We were occasionally invited to work inside churches or synagogues, helping leadership teams or community members develop the skills to have hard conversations. These projects, squeezed among the executive team facilitations and corporate education workshops, felt particularly meaningful to me. But they had usually been brief, one-day projects. Ann opened the door to doing something deeper and more sustained.

A few months later, I got off the plane in St. Louis, and Ann blurted out, "I thought you'd be older," fast-tracking us to both honesty and friendship. Ann admitted that when she first read *Difficult Conversations* she shrugged and tossed it aside. It seemed obvious. Nothing new. "It was only later, when I circled back to it because I was looking for a text to use in teaching that I re-read it," Ann said. "And I suddenly thought, 'Oh. What if I actually *did* these things? What if I actually *practiced* them? What would *happen*?'"

Indeed. The ideas are simple. It's the practice that's hard. Making the choice to be open or curious when what you feel is threatened and furious. Negotiating with yourself to let go of controlling the outcome and instead praying yourself into a sliver of receptiveness.

And that's what I watched Ann and her colleagues do. I watched as they explored the nature of truth, the nature of God, and how it should inform their discussions about everything from liturgy to lunch. I watched as they strived to better understand each other and themselves. I watched them reframe their conflicts as catalysts for growing in faith and fellowship. It wasn't always easy or entirely successful. It was always fruitful and done with prayer and grace.

In this book Ann has put in place twelve *practices*. Twelve attitudes with actions that—if we take them seriously, if we are able to *do* them—will not only transform our relationships with each other in Christian communities, our families, and our workplaces but will bear powerful witness to the world of Christ's redeeming love.

The world so needs this glimpse of Christ. As Roger Fisher, the founder of the Harvard Negotiation Project and my friend and mentor often said, "Conflict is a growth industry. How we wish we could put ourselves out of business." Instead, today we need an assembly of words to describe the conflicts that riddle our world: insurgencies, uprisings, revolts, clashes, quarrels, demonstrations, struggles, separations, skirmishes, stand-offs, estrangements. Even in relatively peaceful and prosperous places our conflicts with each other in the kitchen, the classroom, or the conference room bring many of our darkest days. It's in those very places where the light of Christ can burn the brightest.

Putting into practice the habits Ann Garrido describes in this book will radiate his presence, attract attention, create curiosity, and draw others near.

Ann reached out to me asking for help. But I am the one who has been helped and grown the most from our friendship and work together over the last eight years. At the Harvard Negotiation Project our work is focused on one guiding question: *What works?* I have spent more than two decades in the secular world teaching people skills, tools, and frameworks because *they work* and they are *sound strategy.* The fact that the philosophy and approach also aligned closely with my faith? That was a bonus.

But through Ann, I have come to see that it's the other way around. These practices work because they flow from God's wisdom and his wishes for how we are to treat each other. They work because they are the very practices God engages in his relationship with us. The fact that they can also serve us well professionally and in business? *That* is the bonus.

Ann has broadened my understanding of God, my work, and myself. Teaching people to better handle difficult conversations has long been part of my professional journey, but I've come to see that doing difficult conversations well takes one on a spiritual journey. Situations of loss and grief, hurt and anger—while tremendously painful—can be times of tremendous growth. And the people we meet in tough times—including the people who *make* those times tough—are often gifts from God who can spur us toward seeing something more fully, seeing ourselves more fully, living life more fully. It is in the context of relationship that we become the people God dreams us to be. That is why we are here. At the end of our earthly lives, that will be what matters.

And it's why this book matters. If we take these practices seriously, there is little that matters more.

Sheila Heen
Cambridge, Massachusetts
First day of fall, 2015

Introduction

Christianity is to enjoy a Person.

—Dalmazio Mongillo, O.P.

As a child, one of my favorite sections of the Bible was the opening of the Acts of the Apostles. I loved hearing the story about the thousands of people drawn in by the preaching of the apostles, who handed their possessions over to the nascent Christian community and lived "happily ever after." Hearing my father hint at his struggles in the business world, I considered how ideal it would be to work in the Church with people motivated only by good and holy intentions in an environment void of conflict—the Church painted in Acts.

My first high school job as an evening parish receptionist was quite an eye-opening experience, as I watched four priests of varying generations and ecclesiologies wrangle with one another and with a strong-willed housekeeper to exercise pastoral leadership in a bustling, boisterous Catholic community. It turns out that sometimes keys get lost, the gym gets double-booked, sisters yell, principals cuss, and no one remembers to empty the dishwasher. Not every day, but often enough to leave an impression: the Church is not a place where people live "happily ever after."

1

One of the great gifts of graduate studies in theology was the opportunity to discover the letters of Paul. Written decades before the gospels and the book of Acts were put onto parchment, Paul's epistles reveal a community riddled with discord even from its earliest days. Only a few years after the tomb was found empty, Jesus's disciples were already debating how to handle money, what kinds of public behaviors were appropriate for Christians, and what to do about economic disparity within the group. They had differing views on the role of women, how to handle interreligious marriage, and wages for their ministers. Many of the challenges we know today they knew as well. It turns out, there was *never* a time in which the Christian community was without conflict, and yet, two thousand years later, the Church goes on.

The story I tell of my own journey is not unique. It mirrors the journey of almost every longtime disciple—a pattern of attraction and disillusionment, hope and coming to terms with reality. What distinguishes those who are able to live meaningfully within the Church as it is from those frustrated in their attempts to live "happily ever after" is the ability to function constructively within a church in conflict.

Because it is not necessarily a bad place to be.

Discord, in much of Christian thought, is understood as a consequence of sin: God intended for the world to live in harmony, but sin caused discord. As a result, Christians tend to see the presence of conflict in their communities as a sign of sin, a sign that something has gone terribly wrong and needs "fixing." Because conflict in this view is by definition a *chosen* evil—something we could have resisted but did not—it implies that some party must be to blame.

The Christian tradition, however, can offer a wider, more nuanced theology of conflict. While sin certainly escalates much of the conflict in our world—raising it to the level of violence, bitterness, and even war—the roots of conflict seem inherently structured into the design of creation itself. God created the world with a tremendous amount of diversity and, indeed, seems to glory in it. Diversity implies not just diversity of species and skin color but also diversity of cultures, opinions, and perspectives. Exposure to diversity, with its resulting experience of discomfort, surprise, and disagreement, appears to be the way that God matures creation. Tension seems to be built into the divine "development plan" as a means by which we grow into the kinds of people God dreams us to be. And what kind of people is that? People who can enjoy communion in diversity.

"Communion in diversity." Now where have we heard that expression before? And why is it so important? Because communion in diversity is the nature of God.

At the heart of Christian belief is the understanding of God as Trinity. It is not an easy doctrine to grasp. Indeed, many preachers are tempted simply to shrug and tell the congregation that the Trinity is a great mystery and no one should hope to understand it. And so the Trinity remains, in the imagination of most, a picture of two bearded men and a bird. Fine, as far as it goes, but hardly the animating force behind their lives as disciples. We know that we are baptized "In the name of the Father, and of the Son, and of the Holy Spirit." Throughout our lives, many of us continue to sign ourselves morning, noon, and night with this announcement. But what does it really mean for our lives?

The Trinity *is* a great mystery—indeed, the greatest mystery there is—but this does not mean that the Trinity is unknowable. Rather, our belief that God exists as "three in one"—i.e., "diversity in communion"—emerged because God *did* make himself known to us in the person of Jesus Christ. In Jesus's preaching and in his actions, most especially in his dying and in his rising, we came to recognize that *God is love* (1 Jn 4:8). Not simply that God is *loving* or that God is *like* love. But God *is* love.

Now consider the nature of love for a moment as you have come to know it through your family and friendships. Of what does love consist? How does love function? At a very core level, we might say that the dynamic of love is twofold. When we love someone, we want to be with him or her. We want to be close to that person. We want to be "one" with him or her—one heart, one mind, even one body. Clearly this drive for "communion" is most explicit in the sexual expression of married couples. And yet, it has many manifestations. There is an ancient Persian legend that says that in the early days of creation, the first human parents loved their children so much that they ate them, and God was forced to reduce parental love by 99 percent so the human species could survive!

We continue to see sweet remnants of this impulse in the many cultures around the world that have specific words to describe the desire to nibble and squeeze little ones. In my husband's Chamoru culture from the South Pacific, chubby babies are referred to as *magodai* and are gently bit on the arm or thigh. If one resists doing so despite the desire, they say, the baby will become ill. We simply can't get those we love close enough.

Love's desire for oneness, however, must be counterbalanced by the requirement of separateness. If we are so close that we become one, then there is no "other" any longer to love, and love is not love if its object is itself. The nature of love always requires that there be an "other." How many romances do we know that have ended because one of the partners "lost" himself or herself in the relationship and there was not enough differentiation to sustain the spark? The dynamic of love is a dynamic of inherent tension: the desire to be one while at the same time the need to remain distinct.

In our human relationships, we constantly struggle to strike a perfect balance between unity and differentiation, between communion and diversity. In our relationships, we give too much, we take too much. We withhold too much, we lose too much. When we say, however, that God is Trinity, we are saying that God dwells in this elusive balance. In God, there exists the dynamic of communion and distinction in perfect harmony. In essence, God *is* right relationship. God *is* love.

The good news of Jesus Christ is that we are invited to share in that right relationship of God. God is not a spiraling romance up in the heavens. No, the romance that is God has swirled through the earth, wrapping us up into it. "Go, therefore, and make disciples of all nations," Jesus closes the Gospel of Matthew, "baptizing them in the name of the Father, and of the Son, and of the Holy Spirit" (28:19). *All* are invited to share in the Trinitarian life. *All* are invited to share in the communion in diversity that is God. "God is love," asserts 1 John 4:16, "and those who abide in love abide in God, and God abides in them."

The church properly understood is a school for right relationship. That is not to say that it *is* in right relationship. Our experience of the debacle at the last hospital board or diocesan council meeting tells us otherwise. But it is a boot camp for developing the skills and capacities for relationality that we are going to need to participate ever more fully in the Trinitarian life for which we were baptized. It sounds odd to say it, but the first responsibility of the Christian community—whether it be expressed in the form of a parish congregation, university, hospital, group of vowed religious, social service agency, etc.—is to deepen its members' capacities and skills for friendship, and that includes the ability to manage disagreements well.

Maybe it is different where you live, but where I live we have preached against divorce but done little to train people to listen even when they disagree. We have prayed for peace in the Middle East but done little to mediate conflicts on the staff. We have taken Communion with each other Sunday after Sunday but not practiced communion with each other Monday after Monday.

There has been a renewed effort in recent years to focus on outreach and evangelization by the Church. This is very important. True love is also fecund; it overflows its boundaries just as the Trinity overflowed into creation. But overflow presumes a bubbling center. Mission is an overflow of communion in diversity.

And mission suffers when we do not model in action what we preach is the heart of our faith. "The greatest hindrance to all of our missionary efforts," my ecclesiology professor told me long ago, "is the way Christians treat one another when they disagree." As discussed earlier, that doesn't mean we need to be without conflict, but rather that we need to model conflict done well. Apparently, Christianity is less persuasive to the world when others smell the burned rubber squealing off the church parking lot. But it can be very persuasive when conflict is embraced with grace.

The apostle Paul says that as a Church, we have been entrusted by God with both the "ministry" and the "message" of reconciliation (2 Cor 5:18–19). We don't just theorize about prayer; we are expected to pray. We don't just talk about acts of mercy; we must do them. And we don't get to just preach about God reconciling the world through Christ—the world expects to see some examples of how it is done. Conflict may be perennial. It may be built into the structure of the creation. But that doesn't mean it can't be redeemed. Indeed, done well, conflict can be a spiritual adventure for the participants and a witness to the world.

This book identifies twelve practices for Christian communities striving to live the Trinitarian life to which they've been invited, twelve habits for living communion in diversity well, even when it is really tough.

Many of the ideas herein I have discovered through my interaction with the Harvard Negotiation Project (HNP) and, more specifically, through working with Sheila Heen and Doug Stone and their colleagues at the firm they founded, Triad Consulting Group (www.triadconsultinggroup.com). I noted earlier that it was graduate studies in theology that corrected my rosy-lensed picture of history and taught me to love the Church as it is. It has been my studies in conflict and communications and teaching this material with Triad over the past decade that taught me how to remain in the relationships that matter most to me and how to keep learning from them. This book draws on several books written at HNP, principally *Difficult Conversations: How to Discuss What Matters Most* by Stone, Patton, and Heen, *Thanks for the Feedback: The Science and Art of Receiving Feedback Well (Even When Its Off Base, Unfair, Poorly Delivered, and Frankly, You're Not in the Mood)* by Stone and Heen, and *Getting to YES* by Fisher, Ury, and Patton. These books offer more depth on the nature of conflict in relationship and sound, practical advice for handling tough conversations with authenticity and grace. I keep the HNP books right next to the Bible on my shelf. Scripture tells me what I believe; HNP literature has given me worthy clues on how to live it out.

I have struggled with what to call these "clues." Some of them are skills that we can study and practice. Others are internal capacities that are easier *caught* in a community than explicitly taught. I am drawn to the old Latin term *habitus* favored by Thomas Aquinas. A habitus is a behavioral choice made over and over again with such regularity that it becomes part of a person and characteristic of who he is, an attitude with which he consistently approaches life. Although the English word "habit" doesn't quite capture the fullness of its Latin ancestor, know that I intend it in the classical sense.

My hope is that through making these twelve practices habits in our daily communication with each other—at home, at work, in prayer, and in service—we might grow in our capacity for and enjoyment of the relationships in our lives, because that is what we were made for from all eternity.

In the Gospel of John, Jesus's final dinner with the disciples he had been forming is marked by a long closing discourse in which he relays all that he most wants them to remember before he departs. At the center of his teaching that night is a parable in which he describes himself as the True Vine and his disciples as the branches. Repeatedly, he uses one verb to express what he wants them to be able to do in the time ahead, difficult though it may be: he wants them to "remain."

Reflection on healthy habits for communion in diversity is one of the most important things we can do together as Christians. When we nurture the vision, capacities, and skills for conflict done well, we are proffering a pathway for *remaining* in the Church and in the Vine. We are nourishing the means for living not a life "happily ever after" but "life in abundance"—the kind of life Jesus *does* promise us, even in the midst of our bustling, boisterous communities.

1.   Sidestep the Triangle

If another member of the Church sins against you,
go and point out the fault when the two of you are alone.

—Matthew 18:15

I was first called out on it in the dean's office. I was a student in theology and the dean had often helped me fix my problems—the two courses that overlapped in my schedule, a snafu in my research assistant paycheck. This time it was a professor. Something had occurred in class that was just bizarre—behavior that seemed inappropriate, and I was uncomfortable.

"Did you talk to him about it?" she asked.

"No," I said, puzzled. "Why would I?"

"Because before I hear about it, he should have the opportunity to explain himself directly to you."

"You mean you think I should go talk to him *in person*?"

"It would be the Christian thing to do."

Well, here was a whole new way of looking at the
world for me. It would be the *Christian* thing to confront someone? Someone with authority?

"But he is a professor."

"Mhmm. So?"

Long pause.

"Do I have to?"

"No, but I think it would be a kindness to him
if you would. I doubt he knows you are even upset
about it. It'd be good information for him to have. If
afterward it seems unresolved and you want to come
back, you can, but I won't get involved until you've
spoken to him directly."

Suddenly, I wasn't sure that I cared all that much
about the incident. Maybe it wasn't *that* bad. Well, not
so bad that it merited a face-to-face conversation. I
didn't like what had happened, but I liked the idea of
discussing it with him even less. Maybe it'd be best to
just let it drop. Maybe it would be best to find someone
else to talk about the incident with . . . like someone
who would be on my side.

But after the dean's words, how could I? She'd
nailed a dynamic that was omnipresent in my life
but that no one had ever pointed out to me before:
triangulation.

The term *triangulation* appears to have been first
coined by American psychiatrist Murray Bowden,
a professor at Georgetown University in the mid-
to late-twentieth century. He used it to describe the

propensity for two persons in a conflicted relationship to draw in a third person in hopes of easing the tension. Many since Bowden have used the same term to also describe efforts that draw in additional parties to escalate the tension by creating "camps" of supporters.

In triangulated relationships, there are three roles to be played: the person who initiates the drawing in of a third party, the third party, and the absent party who is the topic of the conversation and presented in a negative light. Although these terms have some problematic connotations, for simplicity's sake, the parties are often referred to in literature as the victim, rescuer, and villain.[1]

Why do we triangulate? Why do we cast people in these roles?

The most obvious answer is that it is easier than the alternative. Most of us hate conflict. If given the choice of chickenpox or speaking directly and honestly to someone with whom we are upset, we'd choose chickenpox.

We rationalize our avoidance by saying things like, "It wouldn't do any good," "It's not worth bringing up," or "It'll blow over." But the reality is that direct conversation is awkward. It is anxiety-producing. And besides, conflict makes us feel lousy not just about the other person but about *ourselves*. The more times I can tell the story aloud from my point of view to someone sympathetic, the clearer it becomes in *my* head as to why I did what I did and how I had only the best of

intentions. The messy details about me get sanitized. I
want the third party to tell me that I am not the problem so that I can begin to live comfortably with *myself*
again.

Research postulates, however, an additional
hypothesis: triangulation pollinates most freely in fields
that are hard to till. Clinical psychologist Ted Dunn
observes: "Victims and rescuers resort to such informal
structures because, for whatever reason, the formal
structures of an organization have failed to provide
them with the kind of influence they need or think they
deserve. . . . Conflicts go underground and cannot be
openly or successfully addressed. The formal structures
and channels are no longer used or trusted as venues
for the real conversations."[2]

In sum, Dunn concludes, "There are two general
conditions that give rise to the formation of triangles:
(1) conflict avoidance and (2) a covert attempt to garner
power through others."[3]

Dunn's observation helps illumine why triangulation appears as the modus operandi in so many Christian communities. As described in the introduction, we
are socialized from infancy to associate conflict with
sin—i.e., always to be avoided. But furthermore, we
worship and live in a larger structure where certain
voices have more weight than others, not just by hap-
penstance but often by design. For better or worse,
ordained and lay members of the Church, male and
female members of the Church, and older and younger

members of the Church have differing degrees of access to the formal structures and channels of the Church where decisions are made, thereby creating an environment in which alternative modes of attempted influence flourish. I suspect the greater the sense of exclusion from decision-making power in a community, the greater the temptation to triangulate conflict.

So if triangulation is a creative way by which we can avoid having uncomfortable conversations with each other and still have some influence in the community, why stop? Because triangulation comes with tremendous costs. As my dean first made clear to me, it violates human dignity because it doesn't give one the opportunity to explain one's own actions or to hear what is being said by others. It violates the principle of subsidiarity that encourages problems to be addressed at the lowest level possible, by the people most directly involved, before others are brought into the picture. And, finally, it has costs for the wider community. It spreads mistrust, discontent, and often division, creating a toxic atmosphere. Problems aren't addressed and solved but linger like a low-grade fever. As a colleague once observed after I'd liberally vented all my irritations, "Ann, you want your anger to be like a coursing stream and not a finely diffused mist."

Given those costs, the better question to ask might be: Is there a way to become more comfortable at directly addressing conflict and more capable of exerting influence in transparent ways? That will be the topic of the remainder of this book. But first, what to do when you realize you are in a triangle as victim, rescuer, or villain?

When You Are the Victim

All of us get frustrated and angry at one time or another, and it is totally normal to share those feelings with close family members and friends. What makes it problematic is when the third party we share those stories with is also connected in some way with the villain in our episode, especially if we are asking this third party to take sides or get involved in the conflict in some way.

The spiritual challenge for the victim entails gathering your courage as best as you can to go talk directly to the person who has hurt or angered you. If that frightens you to the core and you want to talk to someone else about it first to get some coaching for how to have the conversation, that is fine, but give yourself the following parameters for the conversation:

- Don't say anything *about* the absent party that you wouldn't be willing to share *with* the absent party directly.

- Keep the focus on what *you* might do in the relationship, not what the third party or absent party might do.

- Ask the third party to help you see how you might be contributing to the conflict. What do they see about that you might not be able to see?

If you find yourself frequently playing the role of the victim in life's narrative, you might want to ask yourself why that is:

- Do you have a pattern of picking friends who will take sides with you or who will do things you don't want to do for yourself?

- Do you frequently find yourself feeling as if you lack power or choice (e.g., *It doesn't matter what I say or do, they are going to do what they want*" or "*I didn't have a choice*" or "*What was I supposed to do?*")?

- Were there messages you received while growing up that suggested you couldn't do things on your own and needed outside help?

When You Are the Rescuer

Humans naturally turn to others in times of need— at home, in the workplace, at church, or in the pub. Basic kindness means that we try to help each other out, with a particular eye toward those who might be disadvantaged or treated unfairly. It becomes problematic when you are asked to take sides in a person's struggle, especially if it is a repeated request or if you are asked to use your power to influence the outcome in one direction or another.

As one who is being asked—explicitly or implicitly—to function in the role of a rescuer, the temptation is to get directly involved in the conflict oneself. Be careful not to confront on behalf of another. No matter how sympathetic you are to his story, don't make the victim's problem your own. Likewise, avoid setting yourself up as the arbitrator who goes to listen also to the other side's point of view so that you can make up your mind about who's right and who's wrong and how it should get worked out.

The spiritual challenge for the rescuer is to rouse the courage necessary to set boundaries, opting for one of two equally worthy possibilities. One is to abdicate your role in the triangle by letting the person know you are uncomfortable in the role and/or encouraging the person to speak directly with the absent party (e.g., *"I love being friends with both of you and don't want to find myself in the middle"* or *"Have you talked to him directly? Seems like this would be a really important thing to let him know."*)

The other option, if you feel up for it, is to play the role of coach, helping the victim get to the point where he or she can directly engage the one who has done the harm (or is at least perceived to have done so). Coaching, as distinguished from rescuing, is characterized by adhering to these guidelines:

- It's fine to name feelings you hear the other person expressing (e.g., *"I can hear you are really angry/upset/*

hurt") but don't take sides or express an opinion about the situation itself.

- Don't say anything about the absent party that you aren't willing for that party to hear you say. The victim will be tempted to repeat anything you say that bolsters their case (e.g., "*Well, Juan says what you did was unconscionable*").

- Keep the focus on what the victim might do to help repair the relationship, not what you or the absent party might do.

- Freely acknowledge that the victim can take your suggestions or not. After discussing all the options, they decide what they want to do next.

If you are someone in a leadership role to whom both persons report (or the parent of two squabbling children), you might by virtue of your role need to get involved in the conflict. As a general principle, however, consistently convey that you won't get involved until they've first tried to talk about it themselves. If someone feels unsafe in doing so, you can even offer to sit with her as she brings it up, but you won't be sharing her story for her.

If you find yourself frequently being called upon to play the role of rescuer in life's dramas, it is again good to ask why:

- Do you have a pattern of choosing companions with many needs? What does it mean to you that others come to you so often?

- Is your desire to help others getting in the way of them learning to help themselves?

- Is the role of fixer one that you have played since childhood? Who modeled it for you?

When You Are the Villain

Wow—no one likes to find out that he is starring as the villain in someone's story, and yet all of us at one point in time or another find our name on the playbill in forty-eight-point font. You aren't on the stage yet, but knowing that you are about to be can be quite anxiety-producing in itself.

Upon receiving news of others' discontent through a third party, the spiritual challenge of the villain is to invite direct conversation and *only* direct conversation:

- Express your desire that the victim come talk with you directly (e.g., "It sounds like she is upset. I hope she will come see me directly about that").

- Do not consent to using the third party as a go-between by asking her to return a message back to the victim.

- Do not say anything about the victim or share your version of the conflict with the third party. If you need to find a coach, find your own coach (not rescuer) who is disconnected to the situation.

- If you have been avoiding a conversation with the victim, initiate direct communication.

One of the most courageous villains I have ever met was the new pastor of a parish who was having difficulty with the longtime parish council. At council meetings, the pastor and council members would placidly discuss agenda topics with the members showing great deference to the pastor, but then after the meeting the pastor would look out the window as the council members walked to their cars and stood in the parking lot speaking in small groups for another hour. The next time the council was scheduled to meet, the pastor moved the table and chairs out of the rectory and into the middle of the parking lot, saying that he thought "it would be better to gather out here, since this is where the real meeting is." To this day, the event is recounted with much laughter, but it marked a definite shift in the usual patterns of communication within the parish.

I have yet to meet anyone who self-identifies as a villain in his or her own plot, but if it is a role that you find yourself cast in over and over again by others, it is something worth paying attention to. Consider these questions:

- Is there feedback people have tried to give you that you aren't paying attention to? Are there other reasons people may have difficulty approaching you?

- To whom can you turn for honest feedback about your own blind spots? Is there someone who could help you see the role you are playing in the tension?

The Problem That Isn't

One of the most frequently asked questions I receive when working with church groups about conflict has to do with power differential. We are willing to admit the desirability, indeed advantages, of speaking to one another directly about our tensions . . . until we begin to talk about our pastors, our bosses, or our bishops. Then the anxiety about having direct conversation skyrockets anew because the imagined costs become so high: We may lose our job, our faculties, our program—geez, who knows?—our hope of eternal salvation. We consider authority an exception to the rule and boomerang back to the notion that triangulating is the way to go. This perception is so pervasive and there is enough to say about the topic that it merits more extensive exploration in chapter 6, but for now, suffice it to say that none of us is off the hook when it comes to accountability for how we handle ourselves in conflict, even if the villain in our scenario is the pope.

The Problem That Is

The other most frequently asked question has to do with abuse: Do you still recommend direct conversation if the victim has been treated with violence or cruelty by the other, or even if he or she *fears* the other might become violent or cruel? The answer is *no*. But if you are the third party called upon in such a scenario, neither do you want to embrace the role of rescuer and confront the absent party yourself. Scenarios such as domestic violence, sexual assault, or child abuse need to be referred to trained counselors and legal authorities. We need to recognize where our own abilities to coach someone have reached their limits. In such cases the best thing we can do is to help the person find someone who knows what next steps need to be taken.

Even in cases where there is not a pattern of abuse, it might still make sense to get outside help. There are conflicts that are so entrenched, with such long histories or in such a state of impasse, that the victim is likely never going to feel ready to go into the conversation on his own without some additional support. Mediators are neutral third parties who are in no way connected to the conflict at hand and can create a safe, confidential space for all parties involved to express themselves and problem solve.

Most of the conflicts we will encounter, however, will not be of this more severe nature. Most will be the everyday mishmash of forgotten soccer practice

pickups, work schedules double booked, budget mishaps, and botched dinner plans. They will be provoked
by decisions on which we were not consulted, random
changes to which no one alerted us, and professors who
make strangely quirky comments in class. And, as ordinary as these conflicts are, they are the places where
we have the opportunity to offer profound Christian
witness in the way we choose to handle them.

Once upon a time, my dean let me know it was
time to start dealing with these conflicts directly—with
charity and curiosity. And I did go (knees quaking)
to knock on my professor's door. He answered and
we talked. I don't really remember the content of that
conversation anymore; indeed, I don't really remember
the nature of the original argument. But I remember
that I tried something new that day. I became just a
little bit braver. And that has made all the difference
in the world.

Companion for the Journey: **Leo the Great**

It is one of the great mysteries of Christian history:
what exactly happened between Pope Leo and the
infamous Hun general Attila in the summer of AD 452?

Attila had had his sights set on Rome for some
time. The self-titled *Flagellum Dei* ("Scourge of God")
had spent the previous two years attacking city after
city in what would now be France and northern Italy,

plundering monasteries and churches, razing towns, raping women, and killing peasants and bishops alike. His empire at that time already stretched outward from the Hun capital (near modern-day Budapest) as far east as Kazakhstan, as far north as Lithuania, and as far west as Germany, but his appetite for land and power still remained. Rome, capital of the ailing western Roman Empire, seemed ripe for the picking.

To make matters worse, Honoria—the elder sister of the western Roman emperor, Valentinian III—sent Attila a letter. Upset with the choice of husband her brother proposed for her, she decided to mail Attila her engagement ring and a plea for help. (Talk about triangulation!) Attila read the gesture as an invitation to marriage and demanded from Valentinian half of the western empire's territory as a dowry. The letter appeared to give Attila a legitimate excuse to attack.

At his wits' end, Valentinian asked Leo, the bishop of Rome, to travel with two other government officials—Avienus and Trygetius—to beg for peace. One *could* say that Leo was a third party, asked to get involved in what rightfully should have been Valentinian's task to address. But, by this point in history, the Roman government was very weak and the Church had assumed a greater and greater role in meeting the everyday needs of the Roman population. In many ways, Leo *was* the functioning leader of the city and his concern for his flock is well documented.

The mission appeared to have little chance of success. Other envoys, including bishops trying to save their cities, had been killed by Attila in the recent past. And what motive would Attila have to change his mind? He was backed up by an army estimated at around a half-million men.

Nevertheless, the trio led by Leo mustered up all their courage and headed north to speak with Attila directly. They met with him in his tent along the banks of the River Mincio, about halfway between modern-day Milan and Venice. No one knows what was said, but immediately afterward, Attila abandoned his battle plans and withdrew. Rome was spared.

Some have suggested that Leo offered Attila a large sum of money. Some have thought Attila's sizeable army was running short on food and plagued by malaria and ready to go home. Ancient legend, transformed into art by the Renaissance painter Raphael, says that when Leo met with Attila, Saints Peter and Paul hovered with bare swords behind him. But others have said it was merely the inner strength of Leo himself that Attila found so persuasive. The earliest known commentator on the event, Prosper of Aquitaine, writes, "For when the king had received the embassy, he was so impressed by the presence of the high priest that he ordered his army to give up warfare and, after he had promised peace, he departed beyond the Danube."[4]

Perhaps *what* exactly Leo said is much less important than that he was there. He had the courage to go directly to speak with one whom millions rightfully feared and believed that talking could make a difference. Indeed, he bet his life on it.

For **Reflection** *and* **Prayer**

1. What types of conflicts in your life do you find most difficult to address directly? Why?

2. Who most frequently appears as the villain in the story you tell of your life right now? When you think about talking to this person directly about the challenges of the relationship, what do you fear? What would help you feel more confident going into the conversation?

3. Can you think of a time when you were part of a triangle created by someone else? If you were to find yourself part of this triangle again, what could you do to set clearer boundaries and step out of the role into which you were cast?

4. What is one insight you would want to take from the life of Leo the Great regarding overcoming fears of direct communication?

Across all of history, O Lord,
your angels and prophets have greeted the
     quivering
with one consistent message: "Do not be afraid."
As I quiver now before the prospect of entering
     into a challenging conversation,
I need you to whisper those words again in my
     ear.
Give me the resolve to break out of the endless
     cycle of talking "about" this person
and the courage to start talking directly to him
     (her).
Lift my chin and steady my knocking knees
as I walk toward my own meeting "on the banks of
     the River Mincio"
knowing that you are with me every step of the
     way.
Amen.

2.   Be Curious

Truth is eternal. Our knowledge of it is changeable. It is disastrous when you confuse the two.

—Madeleine L'Engle

Truth is a weighty word in the Christian tradition. Throughout the scriptures, the Gospel is referred to as "the word of truth."[1] Christians are instructed in John's gospel that "those who do what is true come to the light."[2] Indeed, Jesus refers to himself as "the way, the truth, and the life,"[3] and the Holy Spirit is called "the Spirit of truth."[4]

Truth is also a weighty word when we talk about conflict, for it often appears to be at the crux of it. Whether the argument is about doctrinal matters or who left the heat on overnight in the school gym, we hear phrases like "That's just not true," "That's a lie," or "Let me tell you the real story."

Given how important truth is to people of faith, claims about "what's true" and "what's not" are likely to send off extra sparks when conflict emerges in the Church. It feels as if one side is not only being accused of being out of touch with reality, but somehow also out of touch with God. What are we to do when truth appears to be at stake in a disagreement?

If we were to draw our models of response from popular media, we would seem to be limited to two possibilities:

The first is what we might call the The Truth approach. Such a stance assumes that there is such a thing as truth, that it is possess-able, and that I have it. The purpose of conflict is to persuade the other party to see the error of his ways and arrive at The Truth.

The second is what we might call the My Truth approach, in which it is claimed that there really is no such thing as truth, and so everyone's opinion is simply that: one person's opinion, no more or less true than anyone else's. The best we can do is to listen to a variety of opinions, since there are no common standards by which we could evaluate the validity of anyone's argument.

Fortunately, the Christian tradition offers a far richer and more nuanced array of options for considering the question. And while it would be foolish to think the wealth of that wisdom could be adequately summarized in a meager few pages, let me offer just three points from the tradition that might be helpful when building a framework for healthy conflict.

Reality exists and truth matters

From a Christian lens, there is such a thing as reality, and truth is being in a state of alignment with reality. The classical definition of the term, aptly articulated by Thomas Aquinas and still mirrored in *Webster's Dictionary* today, defines truth as "being in accordance with the actual state of affairs; the body of real things, events, and facts." In Thomas's own words: "*Veritas est adaequatio rei et intellectus.*"[5] It is not a body of knowledge that one possesses, but rather a state of knowing in right relationship with reality—in a similar way as justice is not something one "has" but a state of being in right relationship with others.

From the perspective of tradition, reality exists whether we believe in it or not. I might not agree that there is such a thing as gravity, but if I step out of a third-story window, I am just as likely as the next person to plummet to the ground. I may not believe in God, but whether God exists does not depend upon my belief. In that sense, what is true is never endangered by humans; reality is what it is. Humans, however, stand in peril without truth. We may not believe that there is such a thing as global warming, but if it exists, we are going to be impacted regardless of our belief. It is in our best interest as humans that our beliefs align with reality. Our flourishing—indeed, in some cases, our very existence—is at stake. It is important that we know what is real. The big, scary question is: *Can* we know it?

Reality is big and our light bulbs are limited

On one hand, we *have* to trust our capacity to know reality in order to get on with the daily business of living. Our ancestors planted crops trusting the patterns of the sun. They navigated between islands, counting on the predictable movement of the stars in the night sky. At some level, we *have* to trust our ability to know what is real or be paralyzed in our planning, unable to make any decisions. To use an example favored by the philosopher Wittgenstein, what if every morning I woke up and had to wonder, "Do I really have two hands or is that just a figment of my imagination?" We are able to get on with life only because there are some things we take as certain.[6]

On the other hand, we acknowledge that the horizon of knowable reality has always extended beyond what any one civilization, much less one person, could master. The further we sail from the shore toward that horizon, the wider the view of the ocean of potential knowledge before us. And, the more we learn, the more we realize we do not know. Indeed, we often discover that what we thought we knew is not—to use Thomas's vocabulary—"adequate" to the reality we encounter. We think we have landed in India, when in fact we are in an uncharted new world. We think we've understood gravity or God or the earth's climate, and then realize it is more complicated than we first understood. Over and over again, we confront the realization that our brains are too small to grasp fully the expansiveness, diversity, and surprise of the universe, never mind what lies beyond its furthest edges. It is as if reality is a bazillion-volt charge and our brains are sixty-watt bulbs.[7] Or, as expressed in the wisdom book of Sirach,

> Where can we find the strength to praise him?
> For he is greater than all his works. . . .
> Glorify the Lord and exalt him as much as you
> can, for he surpasses even that. (43:28–30)

When we make assertions about knowing the truth, as Christians we remember that while there *is* reality, and we *can* know it (indeed, we stake our daily existence on being able to know it), *what* we know of it is always partial and even potentially *less* reflective of the totality of what is true than it is reflective. Humility is of the essence.

Truth is still worth seeking

So if we are never going to really be able to grasp the whole picture, should we even bother trying?

The Christian tradition continues to offer a resounding "yes!" We will never know all that is to be known. And time may prove that what we think we know is riddled with inadequacies. But, as Sirach continues, "Do not grow weary" just because "you cannot praise him enough" (Sir 43:30). We don't pursue truth with the assumption that someday we will possess truth but rather with the hope that someday Truth will possess us.[8] Every time we humbly open ourselves to finding out more—be it about gravity or doctrine or even the source of another's disagreement with us—it is a gesture toward letting Truth (a.k.a. God) more and more into our lives. The act of persistently seeking truth is what we might call a spiritual discipline.

It is an extremely challenging discipline to hold oneself to, as most spiritual disciplines are. Sometimes life hands us pieces of reality that don't seem to all fit together and indeed appear to contradict what we previously thought was real. Sometimes the best we can do is to hold onto new insights like we hold onto the mystery screws and unlabeled keys kept in the kitchen drawer. We trust that someday it will become clear where everything goes, but for the time being, we must become comfortable with a degree of messiness. In the words of novelist Zora Neale Hurston, "There are years that ask questions and years that answer them."[9] *Years*, not hours.

The fourteen-hundred-year-old Benedictine community has a remarkable way of expressing this commitment to being open to the unknown. Each monk takes a vow of *conversatio morum* or "conversion of life." Each monk makes a lifelong promise to keep changing and learning and growing, believing that ultimately the question marks that trouble our minds are not threats to be feared nor problems to be dismissed with a shrug, but rather the crooked finger of God beckoning us to draw nearer.

An important insight of the Benedictine tradition is that *conversatio*, or "conversion," as implied by the Latin root, most frequently happens through conversation. Critical insights into reality, and especially ourselves, arrive in comments from those with whom we live and work. The twentieth-century monk and spiritual writer Thomas Merton titled one compilation of his personal journals *A Vow of Conversation*. He knew that he needed the wisdom and the rub of a community to become ever more aligned with reality.

A Stance for Christian Conflict

This is all rather heady theological stuff. What does *any* of this have to do with the debate over available dates for *quinceañeras* in the parish? The rescheduling of snow days at the school? Or the fact that the heat was left on overnight *again*?

As we talk about how to engage in healthy, direct conflict (versus the more comfortable patterns of triangulated conflict), the first thing we need to discuss is our *stance* regarding "truth." Rather than falling into the traps of The Truth or My Truth, how do we adopt a stance consistent with the wider wisdom of our faith tradition?

Several years ago, after experiencing increasing pain in my right hip, a doctor suggested for me a tai chi class where week after week, I practiced little other than modifying how I stand. I was taught how to unlock my knees, balance my weight, and become aware of my posture. Before learning how to move, I first had to practice what my body should look like at rest. Likewise, before jumping into a conversation we find difficult, it makes sense to get ourselves into an open, resting stance called the stance of curiosity.

Curiosity is rarely identified as a virtue in Christian literature. Prudence, justice, charity—yes—but curiosity struggles to make the list. This is unfortunate because few qualities serve a life of communion more than curiosity, and all of tradition's deepest intuitions regarding truth point us in its direction. Curiosity is the ability to look at a scenario and acknowledge, "I know only *my* truth, and I don't possess *the* truth, but there *is* truth yet to be discovered, and it's worth striving for."

Curiosity requires the humility mentioned earlier; it presumes it is okay not to know everything and doesn't experience shame admitting that to others. Instead, lack of knowing is a springboard for wonder. It makes the asking of questions and gathering of more information interesting, exciting, and even attractive. It primes one for *conversatio*.

Before ever going into a conversation, there are a couple of questions we can use to do a quick "body scan" and assess our stance.

Three Questions to Spark Curiosity

1. What is the other's truth?
I know what my truth is. I know what happened from where I sit and I know how it affected me. But I also know that reality is bigger than me and what I can see from where I sit. My knowledge of any situation is partial. What I don't know is their truth and the part they have access to. What I don't know is how it looks from their viewpoint, nor what their motives are, nor how this is affecting them. In my mind, I often invent a story that explains their rationale and motives, but naturally I do this from within my own perspective. For instance:

- "The parish has long had a policy about quinceañera dates needing to be set at least nine months in advance, with time slots at 10 a.m., noon, and 2 p.m. on Saturdays. It is on the parish website. They know they are not supposed to book a party venue until after they've received date confirmation from the parish. The Garcias just never think the rules apply to them."

- "The principal is now insisting that we make up snow days during Easter break instead of tacking them on in June. Most families already have their spring break plans made. Bill just doesn't make sense."

When Mrs. Garcia tells the story, however, it is unlikely that she says, "We know that we are supposed to book with the parish nine months in advance, but we don't think rules apply to us." Bill is not walking the school halls saying, "I just do things that don't make any sense."

In our own minds, our stories *do* make sense or we wouldn't tell them; our decisions *do* make sense or we wouldn't make them.

To stimulate curiosity, before entering into a difficult conversation try to write out an account of what is going on *from the other party's point of view*. When he tells the story, how does *he* tell it? Why is he doing what he is doing from his point of view? How is the episode affecting him? When attempting to write out such a narrative, one often discovers that there are holes in the story, pieces about which we can hypothesize but that we genuinely don't know. We can make guesses, but they are only guesses. There is only one person who can answer those questions—and that is the other person.

Go back over the narrative you have written and highlight all those lines where you realize, "I don't really know what he thinks here." In a side column, write down the questions you might want to ask when you talk.

What is my version of the story of what this disagreement is about?	How does he tell the story of this conflict?	What questions do I want to ask him?

2. What if this is not about truth?

The question sounds radical. Haven't we just spent pages talking about truth as being at the heart of conflict? No. At the start of this chapter, we simply noted that it *appears* to be the crux, but it rarely actually is. More often than not, it is not reality that stymies us but our interpretation thereof. We frequently agree on the facts. What we disagree about is what they mean and which ones matter in this situation.

Mrs. Garcia may very well know the nine-month policy. But that is not what the argument is about. It is about whether the policy should apply in this particular scenario when her mother-in-law who has cancer has only just now been able to attain a visa to visit the United States. The principal may well know many school families have already made spring break travel plans, but it is a question of whether those plans should have more weight than the agreement signed with a contractor to install a new heating system during the first week of June. The old system has some sort of faulty trip that keeps turning on the furnace in the gym in middle of the night, causing budget-busting gas bills. If this is not fixed, the school will run in the red again next year.

Rather than framing the conversation as a debate over truth, stimulate curiosity by asking the questions, "What is at stake here for the other person? What are they worried about? And, what's at stake for me?" Is it the facts about which we disagree? Or how the facts are being weighed? Or is the real heart of the matter how we feel treated by the other party? Do we see this last incident as the most recent in a long string of similar incidents that affected us negatively? These are not facts. They are feelings, judgments, interpretations, worries, priorities, and values. Still critically important, but not a debate about "reality."

3. What are my purposes?

In the beginning of this chapter, we noted two popular paths that are dead ends if one is interested in making forward movements toward greater truth: (1) the path that begins with the assumption that truth is already within one's possession, and (2) the path that begins with the conviction that truth doesn't even exist. One of the reasons that both of the trajectories often lead nowhere is that they both lack meaningful or achievable outcomes.

The former is problematic because it aims too high. Success is measured only in terms of the degree to which the other is persuaded to agree with you. It demands unity without respect for diversity. Yet if you have ever tried to talk with another person who is 100 percent certain that they are 100 percent right, you know that such conversations rarely go anywhere. More likely they create reluctance to talk to Mr. or Mrs. Certain ever again.

The latter frustrates because it aims too low. It perceives diversity as so great that there is no hope for unity. The parties can each share their opinions, but no progress can then be made toward an agreed-upon solution or common vision. Conversations that lack any aspiration toward a common understanding tend to become circular after a while. What is the purpose of continued talk?

Persuading others to agree with us is beyond our actual control. We can't force others to listen to us, and we don't have any power over whether others change their minds. But that doesn't mean that there aren't still *some* things within our purview.

Right-Sized Aims for a Conversation

First, we can always find out more. If we take a stance of curiosity, we can always have a learning conversation.[10] Mrs. Garcia may still push to schedule her daughter's quinceañera at 1 p.m. next Sunday. But rather than argue about what is possible or what should have been done, we can find out why this is so important to her and what impact applying the parish policy would have on her family. We can ask about whether she was aware of the parish policy and whether putting the policy on the website is an effective way of communicating with her. Does she turn to websites for information or is this a foreign concept for her? This is all good information for a parish staff to have. We'll talk more about how to make a difficult conversation a *learning* conversation in chapter 3.

Second, we can share our own partial truth with the aim of contributing to an ever more *adequate* picture of reality. Again, we can't make others hear it or accept it, but there is a value in speaking it. Our feelings, our hopes, our perceptions, our lives also matter. As a way of honoring our own dignity as persons, it is worth speaking about these things. My truth is not The Truth, but it will be hard for anyone to see the fuller picture if I won't add my piece into the mix. Bill the principal may not change his mind about the school schedule, but it is still worth letting him know my struggles with burnout by this point in the school year; how much a break in between quarters means to me as a teacher; and about the airline tickets I've already purchased. Often just sharing this information can be healing. We'll talk more about asserting our own voice in the conversation in chapter 6.

Finally, we can always invite others to problem solve with us. We can't force them to do so, but we can be curious about what options they may suggest as a way forward. We don't have to agree on a particular interpretation of the past in order to look at a common future. Could the quinceañera celebration include a simple prayer service in the chapel rather than a full liturgy in the main church so as to ease demands on the parish staff? What are the possibilities for getting a substitute teacher during that week? Standing between My Truth and The Truth we can find many options, and we'll talk more about how to do that in chapter 10.

A Final Question: Am I Ready to Talk?

When angry, hurt, or frustrated, it can be hard to shift into a stance of curiosity. Rather than hearing what's on the other's mind, we want to give her a piece of ours. Rather than sharing our perspective as partial, we want to explain to her "how things really are." Rather than problem solve together, we are inclined to tell her exactly where she can and should go.

We needn't be frightened of strong emotions—they are part of being human. And if we waited until all negative emotions were gone before engaging in a difficult conversation, we would never have the conversation. The moment we are looking for is the moment when our negative emotions are tempered with curiosity. If after doing a "body scan" you find you are not yet able to come up with *any* questions you want to ask the other person, it's a good indicator that you're not yet in a helpful stance to go into conversation. Wait a bit. Not too long, but another hour, day, or week—however long it takes for you to surface at least one question that you realize you do not know the answer to. Remember, questions are the graced spaces where God can enter the picture.[11]

Companions for the Journey:
Dominic and the Innkeeper

Not every religious congregation can joke about being founded in a pub. But members of the eight-hundred-year-old Order of Preachers (the Dominicans) take great delight in the story of their origins.

Dominic de Guzman, a priest from northern Spain in his early thirties, was traveling alongside his bishop, Diego of Osma, to Denmark to help arrange a wedding between the offspring of two royal families. The duo stopped to lodge overnight at an inn in Toulouse, an area of southern France greatly influenced by the Albigensians—a medieval version of Manichean Christianity heavy on asceticism and light on joy. The Albigensians (also called Cathars) taught that the physical goods of this earth—food, drink, sex—were evil and to be avoided as much as possible in the quest toward perfection. Seeing the things of the world as the work of a lesser god, Albigensians denied the goodness of creation, the fullness of the Incarnation, and the potency of the sacraments. At the same time, they had very high moral principles and often modeled lives of great integrity, embracing Gospel poverty.

It so happened that the innkeeper at the place where Dominic and Diego stayed was a devoted Albigensian. While Diego slept, Dominic could not resist a good debate. Into the wee hours of the night, Dominic sat at the bar with the man conversing. Numerous Dominican artists have tried to imagine the scene. In a silkscreen created by the Belgian Dominican Albert Carpentier, they sit with a bottle of wine and rolls of bread between them. The innkeeper leans in, pointing an accusatory finger. Dominic has his hand over his chest as if he is taking in what the innkeeper says. The hood of his cape is up over his head, a symbol of contemplation. Even in conversation, he is reflecting. Both men sit facing each other with their feet planted firmly on the ground.

As the first glow of light was appearing on the horizon, the innkeeper admitted he'd had a change of heart. He'd been persuaded by Dominic's arguments about the goodness of creation and decided to abandon Albigensianism. But, just as important, Dominic had also had a change of heart. He'd been persuaded that the opulence of the Church and the low moral character of some of its preachers were obstacles to the Gospel being heard. The Albigensians had a point: the Church was not living well what it proclaimed. By morning, an idea had been planted in Dominic's mind to found a community of preachers who held firm to the world-affirming faith of the Church but modeled Gospel simplicity and poverty in a more persuasive manner. Truth had won out in every direction.

Dominic continued on his journey to Denmark with Diego, but he never returned home to Osma. Instead he spent the rest of his life travelling through southern France and Italy, preaching and working to establish the Order of Preachers.

For Reflection *and* Prayer

1. In conversations where you have a difference of opinion from others, do you find yourself leaning more toward a The Truth stance or a My Truth stance?

2. What messages did you receive about curiosity when growing up? Was it cultivated or confined? Seen as a virtue or a vice? What would it look like for you to become a more curious person?

3. Can you think of a time when you were pretty sure you were right about something and then you changed your mind? What made it possible for you to shift your perspective?

4. What clues do you take from Dominic de Guzman about what virtuous curiosity looks like?

You, O Lord, are way, truth, and life.
More than anything else in the world,
I want to walk in your truth and share in your life.
But this is difficult, for my mind is small and my
vision narrow.
I need your help to widen my view and open me
to horizons of knowledge
beyond what feels comfortable and reaffirming.
Although I am inclined to think that there are
gentler ways of doing so,
I recognize that this tension that I am involved in
right now is your way of growing me.
Arouse within me an infinite curiosity to match
your infinite being
so that I might always welcome new learning and
new perspectives
as priceless windows into a reality much, much
bigger than myself.
Amen.

3. Listen toward Understanding

O Divine Master,
Grant that I may not so much seek
to be consoled, as to console;
to be understood, as to understand;
to be loved, as to love.

—"Peace Prayer," attributed to Francis of Assisi

The early chapters of Genesis include variations on some of the oldest stories known to humankind. Our Jewish ancestors in the faith borrowed much of the plotline and structure of these stories from neighboring civilizations, especially the Babylonians, but they always changed them "just so." I can picture them sitting around the fire at night with their own children, tweaking the message of the stories to more deeply reflect insights they had gleaned over centuries of living in covenant relationship with God—insights into who God is and what it means to be human.

The story of Babel shares much in common with etiological stories from all over the world explaining why humans speak so many different languages. Placed in the Bible, however, the story also makes a theological point about unity and differentiation. Old Testament scholar Walter Brueggemann notes that often scripture sees "oneness" as a good, but at other times, when people try to unite as one on their own, the Bible recognizes they can become a defiant monolithic bloc. Often scripture paints "scattering" as bad, but at other times, dispersal is seen as necessary for God's plan to be actualized.[1] The starting point for Trinitarian theology, scripture elevates the balance of communion and diversity.

Brueggemann notes that in the opening chapters of Genesis, God gives the command to humans to "go forth and multiply," to make of the entire earth a home. But the temptation of these early humans was to settle down in a cluster and stay put. God needs to give them a nudge to keep moving outward. God confuses their language so that "no one will understand the speech of another" (Gn 11:7). The original Hebrew is perhaps even stronger, using the word *shema*—"no one will *listen to* the speech of another."

Brueggemann says it was not necessarily meant as a punishment. More a "love tap," as my mother would be prone to say. But—wow!—shy of yelling "fire" in a crowded area, there is no way to disperse a community more quickly than to incapacitate their listening skills. The medicine administered at Babel appears to be just as bad as, if not worse than, the original disease.

This is why the story of Pentecost in Acts is so fascinating. When the Holy Spirit moves through the room where the frightened disciples had gathered, they are suddenly emboldened to preach. Their message is heard by pilgrims who've converged upon Jerusalem from many different places to celebrate the feast of the first fruits. What is remarkable is that the pilgrims each hear it in their "own native language" (Acts 2:8). God has not erased their diversity. The Spirit does not return humanity to one common language. But the diversity among peoples is not an obstacle any longer to their understanding.[2] Says Brueggemann,

> Perhaps the miracle of Pentecost concerns a *fresh capacity to listen* because the word of God blows over the chaos one more time. . . . On the one hand the new community . . . regarded its differences in language as no threat or danger. . . . On the other hand, it sought no phony, autonomous unity. It was content with the unity willed by God without overcoming all the marks of scatteredness. And so a new eon begins.[3]

As Christians of the present age, we continue to struggle to live into that new eon glimpsed at Pentecost. We often speak of "understanding" as one of the gifts the Spirit brings, but we forget that access to that gift is granted through the ear willing to listen. In times of conflict, that capacity to listen is easily lost.

Differences again divide rather than widen our lens on reality. We feel as though we are once again at Babel.

The Ladder of Inference

In the early 1970s, Chris Argyris, a Harvard Business School professor, first proposed what would become widely known in the management field as the "ladder of inference."[4] His model attempts to explain our contemporary experiences of Babel by diagramming and describing that almost-instantaneous process by which two persons in the same place at the same time can mysteriously translate the same event in ways that make no sense to one other.

At the base of his diagram, Argyris draws a large amorphous cloud that represents all the data—or observable information—available to us to take in and think about in any given space on any given day. Emerging from that cloud is a ladder with a series of rungs moving upward out of the mist. The ladder illustrates how the human mind processes what we observe and experience.

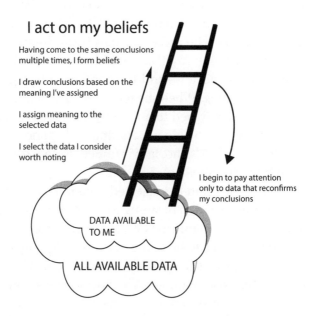

I act on my beliefs

Having come to the same conclusions multiple times, I form beliefs

I draw conclusions based on the meaning I've assigned

I assign meaning to the selected data

I select the data I consider worth noting

I begin to pay attention only to data that reconfirms my conclusions

DATA AVAILABLE TO ME

ALL AVAILABLE DATA

The first thing that the brain does is to select certain data to pay attention to rather than others. Because there is always so much we *could* attend to—the color of the walls, the number of persons in the lecture hall, the smells wafting in from the coffee lounge around the corner, the pitch of the professor's voice, the content of what she is saying, the scribbling across the chalkboard, etc.—the brain has to figure out where to place its focus. This selection centers around a predictable set of factors: our own preferences and concerns, what we've been trained to pay attention to . . . basically, whatever pertains to us. The professor hands out instructions for a presentation my team will do on Tuesday—the first of the semester—and the content of her speech becomes riveting. When she moves on to talk about the presentation assigned to another group for Thursday, the clock begins to hold my attention. That and the fact that the professor's shoelace is untied. Where does one even buy pink shoelaces?

Once the brain has selected data to pay attention to, it begins to assign meaning to it. The professor only spent about two minutes giving instructions to my group but seems to be going on for much longer with the next group. The amount of time spent with each group means something. Why would she spend less time with my group than the others?

Now, the brain moves to conclusions: the professor doesn't care about my group's success in the same way she does the other group's success.

If this cycle were to repeat itself a few more times, the conclusions I draw would begin to become beliefs. I begin to select data that reinforces what I've seen in the past and supports my conclusion: this professor doesn't treat her students equally. She favors some more than others. She didn't laugh at the pun I cleverly embedded in our presentation. She didn't call on me when I raised my hand today. She wasn't there when I walked past her office during her office hours.

And, eventually, my story about this professor leads to action: when she offers suggestions, I have a scowl on my face. When I write my papers, I do so with resentment. I wonder if it matters how much time I put in. Maybe I will write about this in my course evaluation at the end of the semester. If I get a low grade, I am definitely filing a complaint with the dean.

Now, imagine for a moment the professor's diary over the course of the semester:

> *August 15*—Love this new class! Don't know how I will manage grading all seventy-five of them without a TA. Better have some group projects.

> *September 15*—Spent hours over the weekend creating different projects for different groups, trying to keep it interesting for them. May have made one group's project a little too complicated. Took me fifteen minutes just to explain the instructions and they still had lots of questions. Note to self: simplify this next semester.

> *October 15*—First experiment with group presentations was great! First group was so good I had little feedback to offer them afterward to help them improve. There was this one person in the group with mom jeans, though, who seemed a little terse in her speech. Where do you even get jeans like that anymore?

November 15—Mom Jeans just sits there and squints at me. I've suggested moving up closer to the front. Think this person might need glasses.

December 15—No, it's definitely a scowl. No idea what is going on with MJ. Probably something back home or at work. Don't want to put MJ on the spot, so just pretend I don't see it and try to keep positive spirit with the rest of class.

January 15—Beginning of a new semester and the first thing I have to do is have a meeting with the dean and MJ. MJ says that I show undue preference for some students over others and that "B+" was an unfair grade. What??!! It was one of the higher grades in the class! Should have docked MJ another letter grade just for attitude last semester, bringing down mood of the room with that permanent scowl.

Two people, two different ladders. And Babel breaks out all over again. What can we do to draw the Spirit back into this space?

In times of conflict, our conversations tend to start at the top of the ladder. We stand on the highest rungs trading our conclusions and beliefs. Argyris notes that the most effective thing we can do is move backward down the ladder and be curious about what is happening at each other's lower rungs:

- "What data were you looking at that maybe I'm not seeing? Is there information you have that I might not have?"

- "Talk to me about why _____ is important to you. Why does it seem more weighted in your mind?"

- "What did it mean to you when I did _____? Tell me about how you read the situation."

We've already spoken about trying to assume a stance of curiosity before ever going into a difficult conversation. But it is often a whole other matter to maintain that stance in the midst of the conversation. Accusations start flying. People share data and you think, "That's not right!" The other party climbs right back up the ladder and you are tempted to follow, all of those questions you've prepared in advance fluttering downward as you ascend the heights to the safety of your pre-existing views.

But as we've also discussed earlier, we can neither control nor change how anyone else sees the world. Nor do we have the power to *make* our way of seeing the world understood by others. The only power we really possess—a power that, since Pentecost, has never been taken from us and always awaits our engagement—is the power to listen toward understanding.

Pentecost Listening

What would it look like to participate in the "miracle of the ears" today like on the day of Pentecost?

Many times when we claim to be listening, we simply are not. We say "uh-huh" and "hmm" on the phone but meanwhile answer e-mails and stir gravy on the stove. A step up from there is listening for the sake of rebuttal. As the other person speaks, we skim his or her monologue for the points to which we plan to respond. We listen for what is wrong, illogical, and inconsistent—with the intention to point this out. Neither of these options requires the Spirit, only ears. And we shouldn't expect any miracles.

The first step toward Pentecost listening involves looking for the logic of a person's speech rather than the illogic. It means trying to discover why this makes sense to her, even if you think it is wrong, off base, or simply leaves out the most important parts. Given the data she is working from—what *she* noticed—how did she interpret it, and why does she see it as she does? How did she climb each rung on the ladder?

A second step toward Pentecost listening involves listening for the feelings that undergird the person's story. Where does this have emotional resonance for her? What is fueling her behavior? Does this event tap into memories from her past about which she still has strong feelings?

True Pentecost listening—the kind that unites in the midst of diversity—requires one further step, often called "empathic listening." Empathic listening involves the added layer of meaning and symbolism. Why is this so important to her? Where does it fit into the larger story of her life and where does she see herself headed? As leadership educator Stephen Covey defines it:

> In empathic listening, you listen with your ears, but you also, and more importantly, listen with your eyes and with your heart. You listen for feeling, for meaning. You listen for behavior. You use your right brain as well as your left. You sense, you intuit, you feel.[5]

EMPATHIC (or PENTECOST) LISTENING (listen to grasp the meaning this has for the other)

LISTENING FOR EMOTION (listen for the feelings underneath what the other is saying)

LISTENING FOR LOGIC (listening to figure out why what the other is saying makes sense to them)

DEFENSIVE LISTENING (listening for what is wrong/illogical in what the other is saying)

CASUAL LISTENING (sporadic listening in the midst of other distractions)

Sometimes people think that with empathic listening you must agree with the other person. No—that would be sympathetic listening. Sympathetic listening is when the listener says, "Yes, you are right to think the way you do!" "Well, I'd do the same thing myself if I were in your shoes!" But it is very possible to listen deeply to someone without agreeing with them, engaging both nonverbal and verbal cues. The goal of empathic listening is that, at the end, you are able to tell the other person's story in such a way that the person would say, "Yep. That is how I see it. That is how I feel about it. You get why this matters to me. You have understood."

Attend to the Nonverbals

The miracle of the ears, as described above, clearly involves more than the ears. As Covey suggests, real listening involves the eyes, the heart—indeed, the whole body. Communications experts often note that effective communication is comprised of about 10 percent words, 30 percent tone, and 60 percent body language. There are a couple of simple things you can do to convey your intent to listen empathically: Make eye contact. Lean in toward the person. Let them know you are paying attention and taking in what they are saying and working to make sense of it yourself. A well-placed "Wow" or even "Huh" makes your engagement more apparent. The quality of your physical presence is as important as your words

Practice the Verbals

Empathic listening can involve a number of verbal skills that may or may not come naturally but can generally be mastered with just a bit of practice. They are simple skills to fall back on when you are not sure what to say next in the conversation but want to convey an effort to understand.

Paraphrasing is the capacity to repeat back the content of a message in such a way that it conveys it was heard.

> *Professor*: The fact that you were scowling at me all of the time inclined me to look elsewhere in the room.

> *Student*: Interesting. So the expression on my face kept you from looking in my direction.

Summarizing is the skill of synthesizing the main points of another's statements.

> *Student*: You gave the other groups far more explanation about the group projects than you gave our group. You took up lots of class time to explain to them and answer their questions, but our group you just breezed by in about thirty seconds. I don't think it's fair that you graded them higher because obviously they had more help.

> *Professor*: You saw the other groups receiving more of my attention in class and that strikes you as unfair.

You can also name the emotions that underlie a statement. This needs to be done carefully since you are never certain as to what is going on in another's body; the best you can do is hypothesize. But, even if the hypothesis is wrong, it can still further the conversation. (More on this to come in chapter 5.)

> *Professor*: I bent over backward this past semester in order to create interesting and meaningful assignments for an enormously large class without the help of a teaching assistant.
>
> *Student*: I imagine I'd feel unappreciated if I were in your shoes.

And of course, asking questions will play an important part in any conversation marked by curiosity. The skill of asking empathic questions, however, is perhaps the most complicated of the verbal techniques. Merely sticking a question mark on the end of a sentence does not make it a question. Even with the best of intent, much of what we intend as inquiry turns out to be advocacy in disguise:

> *Student*: Don't you think that it's only fair that all of the student groups get the same amount of your time?

> *Professor*: With seventy-five students in the class, how could I ever make sure they each get the same amount of my attention? How could one person keep track of such a thing?

Advocacy works for lawyers who are trying to build a case in court and use cross-examination to lead a jury toward a particular conclusion. It does *not* work well in persuading the person being cross-examined. They simply feel misunderstood and manipulated. And it does *not* work well in ongoing relationships—even for lawyers. Indeed, many lawyers report one of the greatest strains on their marriages is the inability to turn off their well-honed advocacy skills once they get home at night.

Real questions are those that you *don't* know the answer to:

> *Professor*: At what point in the semester did you start feeling this way? What does getting a B+ mean to you?

> *Student*: What did you consider when grading group presentations? Why did you spend more time preparing some groups than others?

Sometimes it can help to mentally adopt the perspective of a journalist—someone whose job it is to understand the story as deeply, yet objectively, as possible. The journalist isn't there to change the mind of the one being interviewed but rather to fully grasp the interviewee's point of view.

A Final Thought: Attitude Trumps Technique

One of the most common misconceptions about effective communication is that it rests in the technique. Many people believe that if they lean in and say "hmm," if they paraphrase and summarize, or if they use the proverbial "I" language when they speak, it will fix everything. They often look for magic words that promise to get the results they are seeking. And they become disillusioned—indeed, sometimes mock the techniques—when they don't seem to work. Upon further questioning, what becomes clear is that, while they were trying on the words, they had not adopted the attitude.

Alas, you can't fake curiosity. Even if you use all of the nonverbal and verbal techniques described above, if you aren't actually interested in what the other person has to say, you will likely come across as demeaning or patronizing. The approaches described are meant to help someone who really *is* curious to communicate effectively their curiosity. The same approaches will be counterproductive for one who is not.

Now here's the great news: if you really *do* want to listen to the other yet you forget all of the tips described in this chapter, you will still be fine. If you are genuine in your desire to understand, you will sometimes stumble on your words. You will sometimes say things that you wish you didn't say. The other person will accuse you of not understanding. And all of this is okay. All that you need to do is remain curious and say, "Tell me more." In doing so, you keep open that space for the Spirit to enter and for a miracle of the ears to occur.

Companions for the Journey:
Francis and Malik al-Kamil

People around the globe recognize the brown robes and telltale bird of Francis of Assisi, perhaps the most beloved of all Christian saints. He is known as the lover of animals, singer of canticles, and champion of simplicity. But forerunner of Muslim-Christian dialogue?

The story of Francis's encounter with Malik al-Kamil is among the lesser known in the saint's lore. Yet, in light of the tensions of this century, it seems to possess increased relevance and hope for it testifies to the power of "Pentecost listening" even in the most extreme circumstances.

As a citizen of the thirteenth century, Francis knew something about war. While still a teen, he was involved in a local battle between his native Assisi and the neighboring Perugia that led to his capture and imprisonment for a year. Francis's personal experience of war sparked the beginning of a conversion in his own life away from the familiar toward the *other*, away from all forms of violence toward peace. Ever so slowly his conversion shifted his focus from the hills of Umbria to the lands beyond the Mediterranean Sea.

In the years following the official founding of the Franciscan order in 1209, Francis found himself increasingly drawn toward engagement with the Muslim faith. Twice he tried unsuccessfully to cross the Mediterranean to initiate conversation with Muslim leaders. Once his ship blew off course and once he was unable to gain access to the sultan in Morocco.[6] Then, on the eve of the Fourth Lateran Council in 1213, Pope Innocent III called for another crusade—the fifth in a long series of devastating battles waged between Christian and Muslim armies over possession of Jerusalem and surrounding territories.

Historians are of mixed mind about Francis's intentions when he appeared in battle-torn Damietta, Egypt, in 1219. Was he hoping to contribute to a peace process? Cardinal Pelagius, the Church leader organizing the military campaign against the sultan in Egypt, had not asked nor supported Francis to take on this task. Did he just want to speak with the sultan about the Gospel? The timing hardly seemed promising given the sultan's kingdom was under attack by Christian forces. It would almost appear that Francis had come seeking martyrdom, for it seemed the only likely outcome.[7] Nevertheless, in early September of that year, Francis and fellow friar Illuminato intentionally approached the sultan's encampment, knowing full well they would be arrested by his guards.

Remarkably, they were not killed immediately but instead taken before the sultan himself. A multi-day conversation between the men ensued.

Perhaps the most notable part of this story is not that Francis spent so much time listening to the sultan but rather that the sultan spent so much time listening to Francis. Malik al-Kamil was the nephew of Saladin, whose army had conquered Jerusalem from the Christian militia in the third crusade. The son of one of the most powerful men in the whole Middle East, he had ruled Egypt since the age of twenty. He had no reason to entertain Francis's presence. Yet, Malik al-Kamil also had a reputation of being religiously tolerant of Christians and Jews and providing for prisoners of war in unexpectedly generous ways.[8] Although Francis's words likely made little sense to him, Francis's attitude of humble curiosity impressed him.

Jacques de Vitry, the first to write of this event, says that when Malik al-Kamil saw Francis dressed in his customary rags, "he recognized him as a man of God and changed his attitude into one of gentleness, and for some days he listened very attentively to Francis as he preached the faith of Christ to him and his followers."[9]

Neither Francis nor Malik al-Kamil were moved to change their religious affiliations from the encounter, nor did the crusade end as a result of their dialogue. Indeed, the war-weary region endured many more years of violence extending beyond the lifetimes of both men. But conversion has many dimensions, some of which are subtle and emerge only over many years. At the end of their time together, Vitry records the sultan as saying, "Pray for me, that God may deign to me the law and the faith which is more pleasing to him."[10] Francis came home with a carved horn, used five times a day in Islam to call the people to prayer. In subsequent letters, Francis urged Christians to adopt a similar practice allowing prayer to permeate their lives.[11] Francis's famous prayer "The Praises of God," written in 1224, bears a striking resemblance to the Muslim prayer "The 99 Beautiful Names of God."[12] Obviously the encounter left a mark on both of them.

And somewhere in Egypt, there is rumored to be a Sufi grave with an inscription testifying that the deceased's life was forever changed the day "a Christian monk and the sultan met in his tent."[13] Sometimes we find out there are others "listening to our listening" who we do not even know are there.

For **Reflection** *and* **Prayer**

1. What relationship in your life right now most seems to resemble Babel? What would have to change for it to become a Pentecost story instead?

2. When considering the ladder of inference, to what kinds of data do you seem to give preference more than others? What significant experiences from your past tend to shape what and how you see now?

3. Can you think of a time when you were able to move up a level of listening (e.g., from defensive listening to listening for logic)? What happened that helped you move to the next level?

4. What do you find most hopeful about the story of Francis and Malik al-Kamil that you would want to hold onto?

Divine Creator,

At the dawn of time, you fashioned an earth over-
     flowing with life.

For six days you labored and on the seventh you
     stood back,

and you listened to the echo of all creation and
     have been listening ever since.

We praise and you receive our worship.

We cry and you hear our prayer.

We lament and you remember us.

Your ear is never deaf to our voice; your face
     never turned away from us.

And now, Creator God, I should like to learn to
     listen like you.

In times of tension, lament, and complaint,

keep my ears open to the rumblings of emotions
     and meaning

just under the surface of the words I hear.

May your Spirit swirl freely through my
     conversations

that I may hear all that you would have me hear

and understand all that you would have me
     understand.

Amen.

4. Undo the Knot of Intention

It should be presupposed that every good Christian ought to be more eager to put a good interpretation on a neighbor's statement than to condemn it.

Further, if one cannot interpret it favorably, one should ask how the other means it.

—Ignatius of Loyola, *The Spiritual Exercises*

Several years ago while visiting the ancient Bavarian city of Augsburg, our German companion and guide slid us into the side door of a church. It was late afternoon, and I had seen so many churches they were beginning to all meld in my mind, but she insisted that we take a moment here. She steered my friend and I to a Baroque painting above a side altar and indicated it was a very important piece of art but struggled to translate the title. She called the woman in the painting *Maria Knotenlöserin* and kept gesturing with her hands the untying of a knot, imitating the action of the woman in the picture who was untangling a long ribbon. As a cradle Catholic, I'd been acquainted with many different images of Mary in my lifetime, but this was an entirely new one to me. As I left, I kept wondering, "Why is Mary holding a ribbon? And what's with the knots?"

I later discovered this painting in the Church of Saint Peter am Perlach was commissioned in 1700 by a minister named Hieronymus Langenmantel in gratitude for a moment of transformation in his own family's history. The ribbon in the painting represented a marriage ribbon, still used in many weddings around the world, in which couples are tied or looped together as a sign of their new unity with each other. The ribbon in the painting, however, had become twisted and knotted, a sign of how Langenmantel's grandparents had come to experience their own married life. At the peak of frustration, on the edge of divorce, Langenmantel's grandfather had turned to a local minister who met with him and prayed with him over the course of a month and helped him to "untangle" the conflicts with his wife.

The metaphor of conflict being like a knot resonates with many people, including, it turns out, Pope Francis, who stumbled on the painting while visiting Germany in the 1980s after a difficult stint as a seminary rector. It has since become a central image in his papacy.

When describing conflict, we naturally use "knot" language. We describe our thought patterns as tangled.

We know we mean to be clear, but our words come out jumbled. We think the issue is one thing but find it is intertwined with so many different things. When we talk about what the conflict is doing to our bodies, we describe our stomachs as knotted, our nerves as taut. We speak of conflict as a "game of tug-of-war"—each person pulling on his or her end of the line harder to try to make headway but in reality just making the "knot" tighter. In the words of Pope Francis, "These knots take away our peace and serenity. They are dangerous, since many knots can form a tangle that gets more and more painful and difficult to undo."[1]

One way of framing the question for this chapter is: How do we loosen the knots? We've talked about going into the conversation curious, rather than "tugging" to bring others to our point of view. We've talked about listening to understand how the other party is looking at things. Now we want to consider approaches to analyzing the knot itself and prying the strands apart. If you've been involved in detangling a ribbon or cord or chain before, you know this often takes a lot of patience and dexterity. Fortunately, although each of us perceives our particular knot to be unique, there is one key cause of entanglement: the attribution of intention.

The Original Knot: Intent vs. Impact

The story of Adam and Eve in chapter 3 of Genesis is often referred to as the story of original sin.

In chapter 2, Adam and Eve were told by God that they could eat of any tree in the garden except the tree of the knowledge of good and evil. In chapter 3, they eat of exactly that tree. Why? Well, innumerable commentaries have been written on that question, but for our purposes, one point worth noting is that immediately before taking the forbidden fruit, the snake plants in the woman's mind a question about God's intention:

> He said to the woman, "Did God say, 'You shall not eat from any tree in the garden'?"
>
> The woman said to the serpent, "We may eat of the fruit of the trees in the garden; but God said, 'You shall not eat of the fruit of the tree that is in the middle of the garden, nor shall you touch it, or you shall die.'"
>
> But the serpent said to the woman, "You will not die; for God knows that when you eat of it your eyes will be opened, and you will be like God, knowing good and evil." (Gen 3:1b–5)

Now, there are many reasons why God may not have wanted Adam and Eve to eat of that tree. Perhaps God thought they weren't ready quite yet but might be later. Perhaps dangers lurked there. Who knows? The original knot between God and humans, between humans and humans, between humans and nature begins when Adam and Eve neglect to *ask* and instead assume they know why: because God wants to keep something amazing from them. Because God doesn't want competition.

In chapter 2, we talked about the practice of spending time in advance of a hard conversation writing out how the other person might tell the story. We explored taking a highlighter to all the parts of the story where we don't really know what the other would say. One of the areas that should consistently glow with neon yellow is that of intent.

We often think we know why others did what they did. In times of tension, we are inclined to assume the motivation was negative.

- "I wasn't considered for the director's role because he doesn't want to hire a woman."

- "The bulletin editor didn't include my announcement because she doesn't support peace and justice (or pro-life or children's) activities."

In reality, what we know is not their intention but the impact of their actions on us: "I am without a job for which I was highly qualified." "No one showed up at the event I spent so much time trying to coordinate." Douglas Stone, Bruce Patton, and Sheila Heen — researchers at the Harvard Negotiation Project—note: "The conclusions we draw about intentions based on the impact of others' actions on us are rarely charitable. . . . When we've been hurt by someone else's behavior, we assume the worst."[2] They go on to say:

What's ironic—and all too human—about our tendency to attribute bad intentions to others is how differently we treat ourselves. When your husband forgets to pick up the dry cleaning, he's irresponsible. When you forget to book the airline tickets, it's because you are overworked and stressed out.[3]

Untangling Intent from Impact

A characteristic of challenging conversations is that intent and impact become knotted together and hard to tease apart. From within the conflict, they look like the same thing. Taking one step back from the conflict, we can see they are quite distinct. As a general rule of thumb, it helps to remember two things. One, we only know the impact of others' actions on us; we don't know their intent. Two, we only know *our* intent; we don't know what the impact of our actions has been on others. Because another's impact on us was hurtful does not mean that he or she intended to hurt us. And because we had good intentions does not mean we couldn't have hurt someone else.[4]

INTENT ≠ IMPACT

MY INTENT	**MY IMPACT ON THEM** **?**
THEIR INTENT **?**	**THEIR IMPACT ON ME**

What can we do when we realize the two are tangled in a situation?

Don't Suppress Assumptions; Test Them

It would be easy to say "just don't assume" and pretend that would solve the problem, but our brain abhors a vacuum in any story line and automatically begins to fill in the empty spaces we don't know with rationales—many of which could be quite sound. So it is not a question of pretending we don't have assumptions but rather of testing them.

- "I am looking to get a little additional feedback on why I was not promoted to director. This was a role I'd been preparing for, I thought with your encouragement, for quite some time. I have to admit that one of the story lines I've got running through my head is that I was not appointed because I am a woman. Can you talk to me about what role, if any, that played in your consideration?"

- "I was upset that the announcement I sent in two weeks ago didn't make it into the bulletin. Could you tell me what happened? . . . I was wondering whether discomfort with the activity itself also was a factor."

Often you will learn that there was no intent whatsoever. They didn't realize the announcement wasn't included. They weren't paying attention. A mistake was made. They had no idea their behavior would upset you.

But sometimes you'll learn that they *did* have intentions, but they were different or more complex than you thought. They have been encouraging you to work toward the director's role and even assumed you were a front-runner candidate. But then someone else showed up with better background for what the role needs right now. They are almost as disappointed as you are.

I once had constructed in my head an elaborate conversation with a coworker who had not responded to a question in weeks, although I'd e-mailed him several times. Although I found the matter pressing and important, I decided that he clearly didn't find it worthy of a reply—which made me all the more furious. When I finally found him in person, I told him what I thought was going on: "You clearly don't think this is worth your time." "Wait," he said. "You think that this *isn't* important to me? No, what's going on inside my head is, 'I've screwed this up so bad and delayed on this so long, I have no idea what to say to you.'"

Well, that made for an entirely different conversation.

Make the Distinction Explicit

It sounds funny to begin a paragraph on intention with the suggestion "be intentional," but there is no way around it: be intentional about making the distinction between intent and impact in the conversation.

- "I was really offended when _____. I'm not saying that you meant to offend me, but I guess I'd like to hear what your intentions actually were."

- "It sounds like you were really hurt by my decision. I can promise you, it was not my intention to hurt you, but that doesn't mean you weren't nevertheless really upset by what I did. Tell me more about the effect on you."

It is tempting to think that if we just describe our intentions and clarify that they were good, the other person will see how wrong they were about us and stop being hurt. Sometimes that works. More likely, we will need to learn to live with the discomfort of knowing: Intention doesn't sanitize impact. Impact often doesn't reflect intent. Both can be true at the same time.

Practice the Principle of Charitable Interpretation
The principle of charitable interpretation has a long history in the world of philosophy and easy applicability in the world of healthy conflict. Simply stated, it means assuming the most positive, coherent interpretation possible of the other's behavior. Recognizing there are many possible story lines to explain the other's actions, tilt in the direction of the story line that would cast the other as competent and well-intentioned.

This is much easier advocated than lived. The world of philosophy identifies the two most common violations of the principle as the propensity to create "straw men" and the tendency toward *ad hominem* arguments.

Straw men statements are statements where we pretend to be taking on the other's point of view but actually only take on a weaker version of the argument—similar to putting forward a scarecrow rather than a real living person. It will fool some but not many. For example:

- "Evolutionists believe that we all descended from apes."

- "Pro-lifers only care about babies before they are born."

- "You want us to cut departmental expenses again this year? So are you saying you value profit more than patient safety? Are we supposed to use rubber bands to hold people together?"

No evolutionist, nor pro-life advocate, nor hospital administrator would recognize these arguments as representing what they actually believe. As many a believer has written in recent years in response to some of the writing of the "new atheism" movement, "I also don't believe in the same God you don't believe in."[5]

Ad hominem—literally "toward the person"—statements are those made about (often against) a person's character or traits to disqualify the person's argument. Sometimes these statements are so malicious as to fall under the category of "attacks." In Church life, these statements are often more subtle. They slip out unwittingly and we aren't even aware that our biases are on display.

- "You wouldn't understand since you've never had to struggle financially yourself (or you've never held down a job, or you've never finished high school).''

- "You wouldn't think that way if you were a woman (or a man, if you were black or white, if you were married or if you were single)."

- "Should we really be taking financial advice from someone who is covered in tattoos from head to toe?"

Our unique experiences and life circumstances certainly influence how we look at the world around us. But whether we are or aren't one thing—employed, married, or tattooed—should not be used to dismiss the merit of what we are saying or the impact of what we are feeling.

The principle of charitable interpretation steers us toward ever more careful, even generous, speech:

- "When I first heard the news, I was shocked. I thought, 'That doesn't sound like the Trevor I know.' And I knew that before I did anything else, I wanted to hear your side of the story."

- "I was really stung when I found out. But I'm not thinking that it was your intent to hurt me. Indeed, I'm betting it wasn't. So tell me about your thinking leading up to this decision."

But Is There No Such Thing as Bad Intent?

Humanity is flawed and we sin against God, fellow humans, and the earth all too frequently. But think about it for a moment from within any given situation. Can you think of a time when you would say that you intended to hurt someone? Likely, if you are anything like me, you thought, "Well, I can think of a time when I had many different motives, some of which were probably not entirely pure, but inflicting hurt wasn't my overarching goal."

For the sake of argument, though, let's just say that you were able to think of a time about which you could say in all honesty, "Yep, I really intended to hurt ____." Take a moment to ask yourself, "Why did I do it? Why did I act on that intent?" Chances are that even in this instance you are not thinking, "Because I am wicked," but rather something along the lines of, "Because I thought it was a lesson they needed to learn"; "Because I didn't want them messing with me again"; "Because in order for this project to go forward, we needed them out of the group." In essence, "Because I thought there was a greater good to be had."

One of the quirks of human nature observed by Thomas Aquinas in the twelfth century is that we always believe ourselves, in the moment at least, to be pursuing some greater good. Now we might be mightily mistaken about what the true good is, and we might be mightily mistaken about what the most effective means of reaching that good would be. Sin deludes us in that way. But even if later we recognize the role of sin in our decision making, in the moment, we do something because we think it is the better option. As only Thomas could say it, "Consequently, in order that the will tend to anything, it is requisite not that this be good in very truth, but that it be *apprehended as good*."[6]

If we recognize this in ourselves—that we always intend the greater good, even if mistaken about what that is—then we have to recognize it works the other way around as well. Those who hurt us usually do so in pursuit of what they perceive to be the greater good in the situation. Again, they may be terribly deluded about what the good is, but their intent, as they would describe it, is not bad. Christ, from the cross, acknowledged as much when he prayed, "Father, forgive them, for they do not know what they are doing" (Lk 23:34).

This is not to say that people do not need to be responsible for their actions or that they should not be held accountable for their impact on others' lives. But realizing that the other somehow sees a good as emerging out of a behavior certainly can heighten curiosity: what is it? What is the perceived good the other is aiming for here? Pondering these questions, even if only internally, is a way of practicing the principle of charitable intent and beginning to loosen the knot in our conflicts with others.

Companion for the Journey:
Jane Frances de Chantal

Christophe and Jane Frances de Chantal wed in 1592. They struggled at first. Christophe's estate in Bourbilly, France, was in grave disrepair, but Jane had an administrator's mind as well as a lively sense of humor, and she was able to restore its financial viability while at the same time creating a spirited, joyful home. Christophe fathered a child outside of the marriage—surely a source of much grief for Jane—but rather than allowing it to destroy their marriage, the couple instead chose to respond in such a way that knit them more closely together. They adopted Christophe's child into their household and then had six children of their own in nine years' time. Christophe retired early from the king's army in order to spend more time on the home front. They came to love each other deeply, sharing a common spiritual life and a shared charitable impulse.

In fall 1601, however, their happy home was struck by tragedy. Two weeks after Jane gave birth to their sixth child, Christophe was shot in the leg while hunting with his cousin and close friend Charles "Duke" d'Anlezy. It was an accident—Charles had no intent to hurt Christophe whatsoever—but Jane in her grief and fear was furious. While Christophe immediately forgave his guilt-stricken comrade, Jane could not. Christophe suffered for nine days before he died. During that time, he had his pardon recorded in parish records so that Charles would not be prosecuted. He repeatedly urged Jane to "respect heaven's providence"[7] and make peace with Charles, but Jane wouldn't even entertain the thought.

Christophe's death impacted Jane greatly. She sank into a state of depression and began to doubt her faith. She struggled to care for their children. She moved back in with her father for a time in Dijon, and then was pressured to move with her children onto her cantankerous father-in-law's estate in Monthelon in order to preserve the inheritance of her children. Miserable, she refused all contact with the remorseful Charles.

During Lent of 1604, however, her father encouraged her to go to hear the preaching of Francis de Sales, the visiting bishop from Geneva noted for his wisdom and gentleness. Shortly thereafter, she began to see him for spiritual direction. Characteristic of his style, Francis did not push Jane to meet with Charles. "Have patience with all things, but chiefly have patience with yourself," he was apt to say. He first nudged Jane not to avoid Charles on the street when she saw him, and then to be open to Charles coming to see her if someone else arranged it. "I want your heart to be gentle, gracious, and compassionate," Francis wrote her, "even though I know without any doubt that it will be distressed, that your blood will boil."[8]

Four years after Christophe's death, Jane finally felt ready to meet with Charles in person and forgive him.

The two restored a relationship with one another. Jane became the godmother of one of Charles's children. Charles gifted Jane with a puppy that she named "Duke" as a sign of their healing. Duke became a favorite companion for Jane as she immersed herself more and more in the work of ministry, accompanying her as she visited the sick and sat vigil with the dying.

In 1610, Jane and Francis went on to found a community of religious women called the Order of the Visitation of Holy Mary, intended to welcome women who were older or of ill health who could not find a home in other congregations. Jane's ability to separate intent from impact had slowly allowed her to move on and find a new life. Jane was canonized a saint by the Catholic Church in 1767.

For **Reflection** *and* **Prayer**

1. What relationship feels the most "knotted" to you right now? In what way have intent and impact become entangled in your conversations with this person?

2. What has the impact of this "knotted" relationship been on your life? When you think about the other person, what most immediately comes to mind in terms of his or her intent? Assuming charitable (or at least neutral) intent for a moment, what else might be motivating him or her?

3.   What do you suspect the impact of this "knotted"
      relationship has been on the other person? When
      you try to answer this question, what feelings sur-
      face in you?

4.   What insight do you glean from the life of Jane
      Frances de Chantal that you would want to hold
      onto when you are struggling to separate intent
      from impact?

God, you know the tangle of my life.
You know even when I try to do good, it so often
      turns out badly.
And how when I try to do right, it turns out wrong.
You know the knottiness of the relationships that
      are most important to me;
Indeed, you even know the complexity of the
      ones that aren't!
So into your gentle hands now, I place the strug-
      gle that challenges me most.
I ask that you bring your perseverance and dexter-
      ity to bear on this relationship—loosening the
      anger and frustration that exists between us
and easing us into a freer, more charitable space.
Amen.

5.   Welcome Emotion

With my voice I cry to the LORD;
with my voice I make supplication to the
LORD.
I pour out my complaint before him;
I tell my trouble before him.
When my spirit is faint,
you know my way.

—Psalm 142:1–3

The poetry of the twelfth-century Sufi Rumi overflows
with inviting images. Consider his sage advice on how
we might think of emotion in our lives:

This being human is a guest house
Every morning a new arrival
A joy, a depression, a meanness,
Some momentary awareness comes as an unex-
pected visitor.
Welcome and entertain them all
Even if they're a crown of sorrows
Who violently sweep your house empty of its
furniture.
Still treat each guest honorably,

He may be cleaning you out for some new
delight.
The dark thought, the shame, the malice,
Meet them at the door
Laughing and invite them in
Be grateful for whoever comes,
Because each has been sent as a guide from
beyond.[1]

I am of stoic Germanic stock and have a general
rule to cry but once a year (scheduled, if possible). Yet
Rumi makes me almost excited about what emotion
might knock on my door next. "Come on in!" I want
to say. It's harder than it sounds though, isn't it? To
greet the multitude of feelings that come with being
human—both our own and others'?

In times of conflict, feelings rarely feel like welcome guests. We are swamped by sadness and confusion, overpowered by anger and frustration, and
walloped by surprise and disappointment. Who wants
to let these in? Our first inclination is to slam the door
and move a large couch in front of it. We try to leave
feelings out of the conversation and suggest others do
the same. "Let's just stick to the facts," we say, as if the
facts are what the conversation is about.

But facts are not what the conversation is about.
As highlighted in chapter 2, where we most often differ
is in our interpretation of the facts, the meaning that
we attribute to the facts, how we feel about the facts,
and how the facts make us feel about ourselves and

each other. If it were just about "facts," it wouldn't be such a hard conversation to have. It's hard only because feelings *are* involved, and the conflict can't be managed well unless emotion is included in the mix.

The Nature of Emotion

What exactly is emotion? Believe it or not, even those who study emotion have a hard time arriving at a common definition. Like Augustine of Hippo when asked for a definition of time, we know perfectly well what it is until asked to verbalize it, and then we find ourselves at a loss. We *can* say that, in contrast to thought, emotion is a distinctly bodily experience; it is accompanied by physical sensation. It often moves us toward some sort of action, be it crying, yelling, or jumping with joy. We may decide not to act on emotion, but generally emotion itself inclines us in a particular direction. Researchers have tried to arrive at a comprehensive list of emotions, and there seems to be some consensus on about fifteen basic human emotions, each of which could have a cluster of related expressions surrounding it, but there is no single list.[2]

While we may pit emotion against reason and see it as an obstacle to good decision making and peaceable relationships, there is increasing evidence that emotion actually serves healthy decision making and good relationships. Modern neuroscience suggests that emotions are our body's shortcut to accessing the wisdom our ancestors have accumulated over millennia of

experience on planet Earth. Our brains are constantly
scanning our environment for signs of "something
critical for our well-being and survival," and when
they spot something they think falls into this category,
emotion is triggered. Persons who have experienced
damage in the region of the brain most associated with
basic emotions (i.e., people who have reason but no
access to their feelings) find themselves incapable of
making timely decisions or relating to other people.
They feel no preferences, no excitement, no concern as
they consider different possibilities, so they don't know
what they want or what they should do. They have no
gut sense to go on.[3] As Rumi suspected centuries ago,
emotions carry important messages worth listening to.

Emotional Triggers

What kinds of things typically trigger emotion within
us? Certainly things that pose immediate threat to our
well-being and survival—things like gunshots and wild
animals and falling pianos—trigger immediate and
strong emotions that propel us toward "fight or flight."
But as creatures who have thrived best in community,
our brains are also always scanning for more subtle
relational signs to which they want us to pay attention.

Harvard law professors Roger Fisher and Daniel
Shapiro spent years researching the role that emotions
played in trying to arrive at a negotiated agreement.[4]
They identified five core emotional "concerns" that
seem wired into human nature. These aren't immediate

threats to human survival but rather ongoing relational interests that we all share to some degree. These "emotional concerns" were not emotions in themselves but values that, when triggered—either positively or negatively—consistently evoked emotion. Their list includes:

- *Autonomy*—We all desire to have a certain degree of control over our lives and our work. We want to be able to make decisions about things that affect us and influence the conditions that we live in.

- *Affiliation*—We all want a sense of belonging, of inclusion. We want to know that we are "in" the group rather than peripheral or outcast.

- *Appreciation*—We want others to notice and value what we do and show gratitude for our contribution to the whole.

- *Status*—We want to be seen in right relation to others based on what we believe has value—be it age, education, place in the family, military rank, years of experience, etc.

- *Role*—We want to have a part in the play that somehow contributes to the overall performance. We want it to be something that we are good at, that we like, and that is valued by the group.

When these interests are met in our families or workplaces or churches, it tends to unleash a great deal of positive energy in the environment. People become collaborative, forgiving, creative, generous. When these interests are somehow pricked, however, the reaction is visceral. Frustration, rage, indignation rush to the surface.

And, while there is no agreement on what emotion is, there is agreement around what happens to the body when negative emotions are triggered: a surge of adrenaline and cortisol flood the brain, slowing down the prefrontal cortex where rational thought takes place. We become far more visual and less auditory, so that images stick in our mind, but we have a hard time hearing or making sense of what is being said. Later, we will struggle to remember exactly what was talked about and in what order, even who said it, yet we will remember where we were and how we felt treated.[5]

On Welcoming Emotion

Thus far we have said that emotion is a constitutive but messy part of the human experience. Emotion carries potential wisdom to which we should probably listen. At the same time, emotion can make it difficult to listen at all. In times of conflict, how do we engage emotion in such a way that we can reduce the background noise it creates in order to better tune in to the wisdom it bears?

Contrary to popular opinion, the key to dealing with emotion in a conflict is not to block it out but, in Rumi's words, to welcome it into the conversation. Sometimes it may be helpful to suppress an emotion—such as when you receive a loaf of burnt banana bread from your neighbor at Christmas and do not really care for burnt banana bread. You work to turn up the volume on your (genuine) gratitude for her kind intentions instead. But even when helpful and prudent to do, suppressing emotion still impacts mental functioning. Whether expressed or not, "emotions consume mental resources," note Fisher and Shapiro, "affect the cardiovascular system in ways that appear to be out of sync with metabolic demand, and can even lead to increased blood pressure in one's social partner."[6] Hiding emotions is more costly than we often assume. As a general rule, it is better to work with emotions than suppress them.

Working with emotions is not the same as being emotional. We all get angry, but there are many ways of expressing anger, some of which are more consonant with the Gospel than others. We all feel sad, but there are ways of working with that sadness—internally and externally—that serve our relationships in better ways than others. While we can't control the fact that we have feelings, we can and ought to decide what we do with them.

Strategies for Dealing with Our Own Strong Emotions

Each one of us has what we might call our own "feeling fingerprint"—a unique set of emotional swirls

that belong to ourselves and no one else. Researchers
Sheila Heen and Douglas Stone note that individuals
differ in terms of their emotional baseline (how happy
or sad, calm or anxious, etc., they normally are); their
emotional swing (how excited or upset they feel when
good or bad news comes their way); and their emotional recovery time (how long the good or bad feelings
last after the news arrives). Individuals can vary by as
much as 3000 percent in terms of how long it takes to
return to baseline.[7] Truly each of us has a "fingerprint"
unlike any other.

It seems important to emphasize this in order to
make the point that our feelings are our own. Okay,
to be fair, they are the accumulated wisdom of all the
generations that have come before us as embedded
in our particular genes. But the particularity belongs
to us. Some of us feel a little irate when cut off on the
highway. Some of us feel road rage. Some of us bounce
back from a snippy e-mail in ten minutes, some after
ten months.

The person who is standing before us in any given
argument is not the one who created our feeling fingerprint. The other is not responsible for the contours,
strength, or duration of our emotional reactions. The
same person standing in front of someone else may not
evoke the same emotions. So we can drop the phrase,
"You make me feel . . ." from our conflict vocabulary.
The only pronoun that rightly belongs before the verb
"feel" is "I."

In challenging relationships, we need strategies for recognizing and handling our feelings—both internally to manage ourselves and externally in the conversation itself.

Internally, the first step is often just becoming aware of the feelings we have surrounding the situation. For some of us this is easy; for others not. Those among us who live in our heads are far more aware of our thoughts than our feelings. Our bodies still feel and still emit all the nonverbal signs of feelings, but we are frequently unaware of it.

Once, early in ministry, I was talking to a fellow chaplain about the fact that my car had gone kaput in the midst of a summer full of financial woes. "How are you doing?" my colleague asked in a variety of ways. "Oh, I'll be fine," I kept repeating. "I know God is in charge and watching out for us." Finally, he pointed out to me the fact that I had slouched so low in the chair, I was almost sliding out of it. "So, I'm confused," he said. "Your words are saying you are okay, but everything about your body is saying you have the weight of the world on your shoulders." I had not even been aware I was melting before his eyes. Before we can meaningfully welcome feelings into a conversation, it helps to know what we are welcoming.

Once aware that we have feelings, we can begin to become aware of the range of them. I have a good friend—notorious for preferring the life of the mind— who, in the midst of our bantering, is prone to turn to me and say, "Wait, I'm trying to figure out which of my two feelings have just been triggered." But both of us know that even for someone who prides himself on having a faint emotional fingerprint, there is much more going on beneath the surface than he gives himself credit for. The most immediate emotions that surface in conflict with another person often are but the tip of the proverbial iceberg. The anger that flares when cut off on the highway is what we see above the surface. But below, there is surprise and fear for one's life as well as the lives of the little ones in the back seat. The irritation with the snippy e-mail is visible atop the waterline. But below there is disappointment, confusion, anxiety. This used to be a good friend; why are we having such a hard time working together? I miss how we used to get along so well.

In the conversation itself, one of the most effective—albeit daring—things we can do is to bring the multiplicity of our feelings out into the open by naming them explicitly. Don't stop at one, but use the word "and" to map the variety of emotions connected to the situation.[8]

- "One of the things that is making it hard for me to listen to you is that I have so many feelings going on at the same time. It would help me to be able to lay some of them out on the table, so that then I can really hear what you are saying, because I very much want to hear what you are saying . . ."

- "When I hear you say that, I feel so _____, and I hate to admit that because I really don't like to admit that I have those kinds of feelings. So then I feel uncomfortable and awkward and _____ . . ."

- "I feel _____ and _____ and _____, and I realize that those feelings seem contradictory, but they are all there."

Remember, it is okay if you don't know all of your feelings right away. It is fair to ask for time while you listen to your body and look for words. Furthermore, feelings aren't permanent. They will change over the course of the conversation and over the course of your relationship. Give yourself the freedom to have a change of heart.

- "You are giving me lots of new information, and I need to let you know I don't know how I feel about this right now. There are lots of things rumbling inside me; I might need to sit with them a bit before I try to name them aloud."

- "Right now I'm feeling _____. Who knows? Tomorrow I might feel otherwise. I'll probably have a whole range of feelings before this matter is done, but for now the most immediate thing that comes to mind is _____."

Note that in each of these snippets the word "feel" is immediately followed by the naming of an emotion.

Just like adding a question mark to the end of a sentence does not make it a genuine query, adding the verb "feel" to a sentence does not assure you are about to name an emotion. Whenever the phrase "I feel" is followed by the word "that" we have slipped from the realm of emotion to the realm of thought, and often the realm of judgment. "I felt angry (elated/curious/bedraggled) when . . ." is naming a feeling. "I felt that you were wrong (right/selfish/out of your mind) when . . ." is a thought or judgment masquerading as a feeling.

Unless you were raised in a home where both of your parents were trained counselors, some of the stuff we are talking about in this section probably feels a little bit weird. Oops—that was a judgment disguised as a feeling. Let me rephrase: when we name emotions aloud, especially in relationships we find difficult, we can feel awkward, uncomfortable, or vulnerable. That's normal. Naming feelings invites the other to know you better as a person—not as a parent, pastor, administrator, or daughter but as a fellow human being—and that can be scary. But it is also what builds bridges where they do not currently exist and strengthens bridges that may have become shaky. Your feelings matter. They are a part of yourself that you are bringing to the relationship. Naming them can be a way of being generous even when you are not at all inclined to be generous.

But here is the kicker: *their* feelings matter, too.

Strategies for Dealing with Others' Strong Emotions

Everything you just read could be repeated here in mirror form: The feelings that the other person has are his feelings. You do not need to agree with them. You do not need to take them on and make them your own. You also cannot change them or eradicate them. They are what they are. But if you are interested in making progress in the conflict, it is in your best interest to find out what they are.

You can control how you express your own emotions. You can't control how another expresses hers. And chances are this conversation is tough for you precisely because she does *not* express her feelings as advocated above, by calmly naming the range of them for you. Chances are these emotions arrive disguised as judgments, accusations, stony silence, sweeping "truths" or conclusions on the upper rungs of Argyris's ladder. The way they are communicated may provoke defensiveness and take us back to the beginning of chapter 2: "That's not true!" It certainly doesn't feel like the other person is offering us a gift of themselves.

And yet, if we can find ourselves curious enough to look past the packaging, their feelings are the key to open up what is really at stake for the other person in this conflict—in essence giving us a way forward.

This requires two really difficult skills on our part. One, as discussed earlier in the book, is to continue listening and being curious, even when everything the other says is triggering our own fight or flight mechanism. The second is to translate—to be able to read through the judgment, accusation, silence, or conclusion to the feeling that lies underneath it.

One of the trickiest parts about translating another's assertions into the language of feelings is that it can come across as patronizing. "Don't tell me I feel sad," the other may respond, "You don't know what I feel!" Rather than directly naming the feeling, it can help just to reflect back to them what you see, posing it as a hypothesis or question rather than a statement of fact.

- "It sounds like you were really hurt / angered / frustrated by what I did."

- "Could you say more about how you felt when I _____? I'm guessing that you have some pretty strong feelings behind what you are saying."

- "You haven't said anything for a while, and I'm wondering what you're feeling as I talk."

    Or, again, as my chaplain colleague did for me:

- "I'm confused. Your words are saying you are okay, but everything about your body is saying _____."

Rather than getting trapped in a debate about the facts of a situation, create a hospitable space for emotion in the conversation, acknowledging the role that it *is* playing whether we want it there or not. Such phrases can help legitimize what the other person feels by giving it language. And sometimes they can help ground highly emotional behavior (such as yelling or pacing) like a lightning rod grounds electricity.

At the same time, if another person is expressing his emotions in a way that feels frightening or intimidating or dangerous to you, remember that your feelings count as well. It is fair for you to say,

- "I really want to hear you out. When you yell, I get scared / anxious / scattered and I can't listen as well as I want to."

- "I understand that you've got some strong feelings about this. At the same time, when you leave in the middle of the conversation and slam the door, I feel _____ and _____. I'm not interested in having conversations where that becomes the norm."

We welcome emotion into the conversation, but we don't need to welcome all forms of expressing those emotions.

A Final Hint

When strong emotions arise in a conflict, remember that they are probably connected in some way to one of the core emotional concerns mentioned earlier: autonomy, affiliation, appreciation, status, or role. We may each rank the order of their importance differently, and when they are violated some of us react more strongly or bounce back from their offense faster than others. But whatever our unique fingerprint, we all share the same core emotional interests in our relationships.

When you or your partner reacts strongly to something that just happened within a conversation, consider which of these concerns may have just been triggered. Is what you are communicating somehow a threat to their autonomy? Their sense of affiliation? Their need for status or role or appreciation? If so, one of the most effective things that you can do is to make a move to honor that concern, even in the midst of the conflict. Often this is best done not explicitly but implicitly:

- "I've been talking for a while now about what I think the best solution is, but as the receptionist at the front desk who first answers all of the calls, you have a lot of wisdom on this matter as well. What are you seeing from where you sit?" (honoring role)

- "You've been a member of this community a long time and have probably seen many bright ideas come and go. How does this strike you?" (honoring status)

- "Even as I say this, I know you are the one who is going to be deciding how to best implement it." (honoring autonomy)

Likewise, when *we* have strong feelings, we can also check which of our own emotional concerns may have been triggered. We may be hard-wired to have these concerns, but the uniquely human capacity to be conscious of this hard-wiring means that we also have a freedom to not have these concerns drive our every reaction. While in the overarching trajectory of my life, I would like to feel affiliated and appreciated and autonomous, etc., I don't need to have those concerns met in 100 percent of my interactions. In fact, I might decide to dial down particular emotional concerns in particular interactions. For example, if I could let go of my concern for status, would I be able to better engage the young whippersnapper who might have some fresh new insights despite his tendency to be uppity? If I let go of my desire for affiliation for a moment, would I be able to make some necessary personnel decisions about letting a long-term associate go?

While we want to create family, ecclesial, and organizational cultures that honor these core human interests, we don't want to be unwittingly constricted by them. And if we have some relationships in our lives where these interests are met, we won't have to demand that every interaction will. It is possible to welcome emotion like a guest and be open to the gift it has to bring but not hand over the title to the house.

Companions for the Journey:
Monica and Augustine

Shy of Mary and Jesus, probably the most well-known mother-son duo in Christian history is Monica and Augustine. Their emotional relationship, as described by Augustine in his *Confessions*, certainly had its ups and downs, but their enduring affection for one another—even when they did not see things the same way—eventually altered the direction of his life and the course of Western Christianity.

Although Monica and her husband, Patricius, had three children, Augustine was both the apple of her eye and the source of her greatest concern. Intelligent and outgoing, he also inherited his father's worldly spirit and unbridled sexual appetite. When he left their small hometown of Tagaste (present day Souk-Ahras, Algeria) to study literature and rhetoric twenty miles away in Madauras at the age of twelve, Monica worried. She worried more when he set off at age seventeen to pursue further education in urban Carthage, which was more than two hundred miles away. But she worried most when he returned from Carthage with a live-in partner and child in tow as well as news that he was exploring Manichaeism. Monica refused to let him back in the house.

Monica had great ambitions for her son. It is part of why she invested so much in his education. She wanted a stable marriage and career for him, but most of all, she wanted him to be baptized as a Christian. Manichaeism, a dualistic religious movement popular among intellectuals, was in no way acceptable to her. Monica's impulse to cut her son off was changed by a vivid dream in which she received a promise that "where she was, there too her son shall be." When she told Augustine this, he quipped that maybe it meant she was going to leave her faith and join him. She retorted, no, it was not "where he is, there you shall be" but the other way around.[9] Clearly, both had strong personalities.

After the dream, Monica welcomed Augustine and his family back into her home, but their differences in faith continued to cause her great grief. Knowing she wasn't capable of arguing with him on the intellectual plane, she persistently asked the local bishop to engage him. He, too, knew he had not the brain power to debate someone as learned as Augustine. Finally the bishop told Monica to leave him alone, but to take heart, "It is not possible that the son of so many tears will perish."[10]

After a short stint of teaching in Tagaste, Augustine returned to Carthage for a better teaching position. This time Monica went with him. For eight years they lived together while he taught rhetoric and continued his study of Manichaeism. We might suspect, however, that the tension between the two remained. When Augustine moved to Rome with his partner and son to pursue better opportunities, he snuck off without taking Monica.

Undeterred, Monica decided to sail to Rome. By the time she got there, Augustine had already become disillusioned with the city and taken a teaching job in Milan. Within six months, she tracked him down in Milan. It would be interesting to imagine the conversation between the two of them when Augustine found his mother and her suitcases at his doorstep, but by this time, Augustine had begun to change. Seeds of doubt about Manichaeism had been growing in his mind for some time and he had begun to attend the preaching of Ambrose, the Christian bishop of Milan. Initially, he had gone just to see if he could learn some new tricks as a rhetorician, but over time he found himself being persuaded by Ambrose's arguments.

Bewildered and skeptical, Augustine continued to find his heart churning, struggling with taking the next step. Monica persuaded him to end his fourteen-year relationship with his partner in order to pursue a legal marriage. (The partner, whom Augustine never named, possibly to protect her identity, was likely a freed slave and hence ineligible for marriage under Roman law.) The move was devastating to him, to say nothing of what it must have been like for the woman and their son. After one final romantic fling, Augustine finally decided not only to be baptized but also to remain celibate for the rest of his life and instead form a small Christian community.

Augustine and his son were baptized by Ambrose in Milan during the Easter Vigil in spring 387. Monica had prayed unceasingly for this day for more than seventeen years.

In fall of that year, Augustine, his son, and Monica decided to return together to Tagaste. Aging, she had been longing to return to her hometown. While they were in the Italian port city Ostia, waiting for the ship to cross the Mediterranean, Augustine reports that he and his mother were talking about the afterlife when suddenly "we touched it to some small degree by a moment of total concentration of the heart. . . . Eternal life is of the quality of that moment of understanding."[11] After having experienced anger, betrayal, worry, frustration, and disappointment in their relationship, their final shared experience was one of profound joy.

Within days of this event, Monica fell gravely ill and died before the ship could leave port. Augustine reports weeping tears of mixed grief and gratitude for the woman who had wept so long for him. He prayed, "You stretched out your hand from on high and pulled my soul out of those murky depths because my mother, who was faithful to you was weeping for me . . . [and] O Lord, you heard her."[12]

For **Reflection** *and* **Prayer**

1.   What emotions do you find the most difficult to welcome into your life and to express? What emotions do you find it most difficult to handle on the receiving end?

2.   Of the five emotional concerns listed by Fisher and Shapiro (see page 93), which ones do you find most influential and powerful in your own life? When you think of some of your most difficult relationships, can you see a pattern of one or more of these emotional concerns being triggered regularly?

3.   Does the notion of bringing emotions out into the open in a difficult conversation rather that burying them seem counterintuitive? What makes you most nervous or excited about getting emotions out onto the table?

4.   What does the story of the tumultuous relationship of Augustine and Monica offer you as you consider your own tumultuous relationships?

This "being human," O God, is exhausting.
I delight, I weep, I fear, I rage, I weary, I lament.
This guest house feels very congested,
and many days I don't find there is much space
for anything new that should come to my door.
But then I open the pages of scripture,
and I find that you, too, delight and weep,
fear and rage, weary and lament,
and this consoles me.
For I know that whatever I go through, you already
    understand.
Within you is a spaciousness that can welcome
    any emotion
until its work is done.
Create within me a spaciousness, O Lord,
so that I can welcome each visiting feeling as a
    guest,
receive its wisdom,
and not cling to it when it is time for it to move on
    elsewhere.
Amen.

6.   Speak Your Voice

Always be ready to make your defense
to anyone who demands from you an
account of the hope that is in you;
yet do it with gentleness and reverence.
Keep your conscience clear, so that, when
you are maligned,
those who abuse you for your good conduct in Christ
may be put to shame.
For it is better to suffer for doing good,
if suffering should be God's will,
than to suffer for doing evil.

—1 Peter 3:15–17

Several years ago, I had the privilege of attending a one-man performance of the Gospel of Mark. There were no costume changes or props, no music added—indeed, no original script. Just one actor announcing verbatim the text of the gospel itself. Listening to it from start to finish over the course of about an hour, the story of Jesus came alive in an entirely new way. Over and over again we heard Mark's favorite phrase—"and then . . ."—with which he stitches together the whole narrative like one run-on sentence miles long. Truly, the Jesus Mark wants us to know is an endless whirl of wondrous activity. The pace continued to build minute by minute, climaxing in the announcement of the Resurrection itself. And then, the drama came to a shockingly sudden close: "So they went out and fled from the tomb, for terror and amazement had seized them; and they said nothing to anyone, for they were afraid" (Mk 16:8).

The actor bowed his head and walked off the dais.

"But wait!" I wanted to shout. "It can't end there!"

Of course, I knew from previous reading that the original gospel did end there. Scholars agree that what now constitutes Mark 16:9–20 was a later addition and not in the same style as that of the evangelist. But it always seemed like such an odd note on which to end. Why would Mark do that?

With the abrupt end of the performance, I found myself thinking, "If no one says anything, this amazing story I've just seen played out before me isn't going to be told. It's just going to die." An impulse erupted within me. "Well, I'm just going to have to speak it myself."

And then, suddenly, I grasped the method to Mark's madness. If the gospels were originally crafted to be performed rather than read, as many scripture scholars suggest, this was exactly the effect that Mark *wanted* to have on the earliest Christian listeners. He wanted them to find their own voices and learn to speak up. The future of the movement depended upon it.

In constructing his gospel, Mark was particularly concerned that the story of Jesus and what Jesus valued not be lost to history. As Christians who see our lives as intertwined with that larger plotline, speaking up—like seeking truth—will need to be a spiritual discipline that permeates our discipleship. In the past couple of chapters, we've spoken about making sure that we hear and understand the other's voice; it is equally important that we find and share our own.

For some people this is not going to be a challenge: The hardest part is *not* speaking. The hardest part is listening when you have *so much* to say. For others, however, inserting their own voice into the conversation sounds as attractive as sleeping with rattlesnakes. And when the conversation is in any way public—like at a meeting or involving a microphone—well, add cobras and scorpions to that bed as well. Even if you are someone for whom speaking up is no problem, keep reading because learning what makes speaking up hard for others will help you get more from the conversation as well.

What Keeps Us from Speaking Up

When we see something we think is unethical at work, when our spouse does something irritating at home, when a friend makes a burdensome request, what makes it hard to say something?

Well, that's easy: because there are costs.

Ask any group about the potential downsides of having a tough conversation. They will not have trouble filling a whole page: "We might never talk to one another again." "It might make it worse." "Less collaboration on the staff." "We'll have expended all sorts of time and energy and it won't fix the problem."

How do they know about all these potential costs? They are not dreaming them up. We've all paid them before on the toll road of life. Each of us has been collecting data about the costs of speaking up since early childhood. We observed how our parents responded when we spoke up as toddlers or watched an older sibling test the waters as a teen. We watched how teachers and principals reacted, coaches and scout leaders retorted. We experienced bosses and boyfriends, pastors and police. And, quite frankly, we've received some very different messages. Some of us have been praised and received gold stars, promoted for pointing out an error that saved money or a patient's life. But many of us have had our hand slapped, been yelled at, belittled, lost jobs, or told we caused our family shame. We are not eager to repeat those experiences.

Linguists note that all speech functions at two different levels: the referential (what the person says) and the relational (what is implied about the relationship).[1] Beyond the actual content of what is said, each utterance deepens, maintains, or distances the relationship between those in the conversation. Those who have seen speaking up damage valuable relationships rather than enhance them are going to be hesitant to bring up difficult content in current relationships they value.

But then ask the same group of people to list all of the potential downsides of *not* having the conversation. Intriguingly, the charts often look mighty similar: "We still won't be talking to each other." "It will continue to get more tense." "Less collaboration on the staff." "We'll continue to spin our wheels without seeing any progress." Silence also has costs.

Perhaps the question shouldn't be whether to speak up or not but rather how to do it in such a way that we lower the risk of incurring some of the costs, or—perhaps better put—that the potential costs (because there will always be some) pale in comparison to what is gained. In the sentiment of 1 Peter, if there are going to be costs to suffer regardless, we may as well pay them in pursuing the good.

Common Challenges When Trying to Speak Up

Anthropologists have long recognized that humans around the world do elaborate linguistic dances when they want something of another, whether that is the exchange of ancestral lands or passing the salt shaker.

In some places and situations, people give direct commands to one another: "Sit crisscross applesauce and put your hands on your lap." In some places and situations, people communicate in hints: "Look how nicely the other children are sitting over there." In between these two ends of the "directness" spectrum are a range of other possibilities, like asking a question—"Would you like to try sitting quietly?" (closer to a hint)—or making a suggestion—"Let's all sit quietly" (closer to a command).

Objectively speaking, there is no one right or wrong way to go about saying what you want. Various cultures have different norms about what is considered the most appropriate and effective way to get one's point across. (I use the word "culture" here in the broadest sense possible—to include culture based on ethnicity or geography but also "urban culture," "the culture of Trinity Episcopal," "nursing home culture," etc.) But this is not to say that these norms are not without consequences.

In a famous 1980s study of "black box" conversations retrieved following airline crashes, linguist Charlotte Linde discovered that in accidents where pilot error was involved, the final communication between pilot and copilot often involved what she called "mitigated speech."[2] In essence, the copilot could see the pilot was making a poor judgment but communicated concern at the level of hint or query (e.g., "It's kind of icy today, don't you think?") rather than straightforward advocacy (e.g., "I want to call the de-icing truck back here").

The study is often referenced in business literature as proof that people need to just "say what they mean," but for Linde, it was not necessarily so simple. The practice of mitigated speech in any culture is deeply intertwined with how that culture views power and status. In popular Anglo-American culture, in which people who've only known each other for two minutes begin to speak on a first-name basis and titles are rarely used, moving toward more straightforward speech may seem like a "no-brainer." But in Asian cultures that have tremendous respect for status, the push toward direct command is unconscionable. As Japanese-born anthropologist Takie Sugiyama Lebra notes, it is typical for Japanese speakers to not complete sentences that they know the other might find intrusive, the assumption being "only an insensitive, uncouth person needs a direct, verbal, complete message."[3] In airline culture, where many pilots have been formed within military culture, status is also very important. In "religious" culture or "medical" culture, we may see similar trends. Linde's key point was that where there is a greater respect for status, there is a greater tendency for the person of "lower status" to mitigate the directness of his speech toward the person with "higher status" in order to not damage the relationship.

I include Linde's research here because I think there are a couple of potential considerations for the

Christian handling of conflict, which often does take place in status-conscious arenas. One, if you have a hard time speaking aloud your read of a situation because you see yourself in the lower status role (i.e., "I am just a receptionist/parent/chaplain/vice-president"), be aware that you may still have very relevant observations and information that needs to be tossed into the conversation. Each of us sees things that others do not—sometimes cannot—see, and there is a value to bringing your perspective to the table. Be aware, as you stir up the courage to do so, that you will likely have the propensity, at least initially, to use mitigated speech.

I have attended multiple meetings in my life where I have encouraged someone who was critical of the proceedings to share her perspective with the rest of the group. Afterward, the person has said, "See, I said exactly what I thought and no one listened to me." I find myself searching my mind trying to remember when the purported speech happened. (Can you tell I am Anglo-American?) The difficulty with mitigated speech is that often you believe you communicated far more than anyone actually heard.

On the other hand, if you are the person with more status in the situation (and if you have to ask yourself whether this is true, you most likely are), don't just wait for people to speak their minds. Many of us would say we have an "open door" policy. We think to ourselves, "My colleagues/kids know they can talk to me about anything" or "The associates/aspirants know they can always make an appointment with me." In waiting for others to speak their minds, however, we may be missing valuable information. Moreover, it is possible others *do* believe they've told us something and—like the pilots in Linde's study—we've not grasped the significance of it because it came embedded in mitigated speech.

Tips for Speaking Up with "Gentleness and Reverence"

One of our greatest fears in speaking up is that somehow the content of what we say will damage a relationship that is of value to us—whether it is because we have affection and admiration for the person or we have respect for her role in the community or because that relationship puts food on the table. We are afraid that if the other perceives us as aggressive, there will be costs. The passage from 1 Peter that begins this chapter offers an apt phrasing of what we might aspire to as disciples: "Always be ready to make your defense . . . yet do it with gentleness and reverence." It is possible to be assertive without being aggressive. Hinting is not synonymous with being respectful, and being direct is not synonymous with being disrespectful. It is possible to move up the spectrum of directness while also expressing respect. Hold on to both values at the same time:

- "I think you've raised some really good points. I'm especially sympathetic to your concern about the effect this decision could have on _____. Obviously, at the end of the day, this is something you get to decide. At the same time, there is another concern that feels important to consider. It is _____."

- "We've been talking about the impact of this disagreement on you. You mentioned it's been hard for you to sleep at night because you were so worried about this. It's actually been pretty hard on me, too, and I wanted to talk a bit about that . . ."

- "Hearing your perspective on what happened has been really helpful to me. It's making me think about the situation in a different way. I still have some questions, though, and I want the chance to also share with you my perspective of what happened and where things went off course . . ."

- "I interpret the feedback in the report differently. I'm inclined to see us move in this direction, and here's why . . ."

A side note, but an important one: watch your body language. Recall from chapter 3 that much of what we communicate, we communicate with our bodies rather than our words, and status is one of the things we communicate with how we hold ourselves. Across the world, postures that make us look larger (e.g., standing up very straight, raising one's arms wide in a V-shape position, sitting with one's legs apart, standing with arms akimbo on one's hips) are perceived to be associated with claiming status. Postures that make us look smaller (e.g., crossing one's legs or arms, hunching shoulders, resting one's hands on one's own neck) are perceived as self-protective behaviors and associated with lower status.

As you become conscious of your default body language in a conversation, you can change it to serve your purposes in communicating respect. If you suspect the other person is experiencing you as threatening, it could be in your best interest to "diminish in size." Sit down if you are standing. Lean in rather than tilting back in your chair. If you want to come across as more confident, you will want to stand up straighter, gesture more widely, open up your posture more. In the conversation, make sure your shoulders are back. Engage eye contact. Even before the conversation, however, there are things you can do to increase your confidence. Social scientist Amy Cuddy has tracked the impact of "two-minute power posing" on the ability of graduate students to get hired in mock interviews. Students who practiced standing akimbo in what she called the Wonder Woman pose or leaning back in a desk chair with their feet on the desk for two minutes immediately before their interviews were rated far more confident by their interviewers and more likely to get the job, even though they may not have engaged these postures during the interview itself.[4]

Tips for Inviting People to Speak Up

Linde's research suggests that people in "lower status" roles in a relationship should speak up more directly, but also that those who enjoy "higher status" should "catch more hints." As a general rule, the more status we enjoy, the less we remember what it is like not to have it. *We* don't think we've changed. We are still the same "kid from next door." We can't fathom why people would find us intimidating or hard to talk to, and we become—unintentionally—isolated from feedback. As we become more and more comfortable with speaking directly about our preferences and decisions, we become more and more deaf to hints and requests disguised as questions. Rather than dismiss mitigated speech, follow up on it:

- "A couple of times now you mentioned ____, and I want to make sure I'm not missing something. Is there something about ____ you think I should be paying attention to?"

- "Say more about why you are asking that question. What do you have in mind?"

- "I could be wrong, but I sense concern—or maybe alarm?—on your face as I'm talking. Could you say more about what you are thinking?"

Eric Law, an Episcopal priest who specializes in facilitating conversation in multicultural communities, has developed a practice called "mutual invitation" that can be especially helpful for groups trying to mitigate the effects of status on their ability to speak freely with one another. Rather than tell people they should just ignore their concern about status (something Fisher and Shapiro would suggest is humanly impossible), Law encourages individual invitation.

Law notes that Jesus did not stand on the seashore in Galilee and say:

> "Anyone who is interested in hearing what I have to say, please follow me." . . . If Jesus asked for volunteers, James, John, Simon, and Andrew would not have followed him because voluntarism assumed that the volunteers already had a strong sense of individual power. Fishermen in Jesus's time were probably on the lower end of the ladder. A fisherman would say, "He couldn't be calling me." . . . Jesus knew this; so he simply issued a direct invitation and they accepted.[5]

As a modern-day corollary, Law suggests that leaders establish a practice at gatherings by which each person only speaks at the invitation of the one who has just spoken. The convener of the meeting invites the first person to speak, then the first person to speak invites the second person, the second person invites the third person, and so forth. Anyone invited to speak may say "pass," but he or she still hold the right and responsibility to call upon the next person. Law reports:

> This process might seem very simple and insignif-
> icant, but the ramifications of it are quite incred-
> ible. . . . [Its] consistent practice enables [people
> who easily "speak up"] to become more and more
> sensitive to others who might not have as strong a
> sense of power. This helps them appreciate others
> not based on their ability to stand up to them but
> on what they have to share and contribute to the
> group."[6]

The more positive experiences that people have speaking up and feeling heard, the more likely they will be to assert their voice again in the future, so that the wider truth can continue to be explored together.

But What If Nothing Changes?

Let's just say that your boss hasn't read the above section and your vestry or pastoral council has never heard of Eric Law much less Charlotte Linde. Or let's say that they have, and you've already tried speaking as gently and reverently as possible about the truth as you see it, but nothing happens. Or let's push it a step even further—you've spoken up and there *are* costs: you are un-friended on social media, seated back at the kids' table at Thanksgiving, ostracized at the next con-gregational assembly, or you are looking for a new job.

The effects of speaking up are never known in advance, nor are they within our control. Nowhere in the Bible are we promised that if we speak up on behalf of what we perceive to be true we will be successful.

Rather, scripture indicates that when we speak up about the things that are most valuable to us there will often be costs to pay. While not everyone who feels persecuted is a prophet, I do suspect everyone who is willing to speak prophetically is going to be persecuted at some time or another. It goes with the job description.

But we don't speak up on the condition that our voice will be heard and heeded, or our recommendations will be followed. Those are nice things when they happen. But even when they don't happen, there is still an innate value in speaking up about things that matter to you. Granted, not everything matters to you. Not every bad sermon is worth writing a letter to the preacher about. Not every goofy thing your spouse does is worth confronting. The virtue of prudence urges us to always be asking, "What would be the greater good here?" Or in more modern-day terms, "Is this the battle hill I want to die on?" But when something matters to you, when something is important to you, it will damage both the relationship and your own sense of personal integrity *not* to at least bring it up.

That impulse in our gut that propels us to speak—whether in response to Mark's gospel or just in response to something we see going askew in our backyard—is an important voice to listen to. It needs to be guided by prudence but also nurtured with compassion. It is a seed that the Holy Spirit has planted. It deserves water. It requires discernment. And it will come to fruition, in time.

Companion for the Journey: **Thekla**

The story of Thekla is an ancient one in the history of Christianity—first recorded in a document called "The Acts of Paul and Thekla"[7] written somewhere around AD 160 and preserved in a particular way within the Orthodox community.

Thekla was a teen from a wealthy family in Iconium (present-day Konya, Turkey) when the apostle Paul came to town to preach the Gospel. Forbidden by her mother from going to listen to him at a neighbor's house, she instead listened from her window for three days and was by his words wooed not only to Christianity but also to lifelong celibacy for the sake of the kingdom of God. The option seemed to open up doors for her as a woman that she had never imagined before. She could have a voice about her future. She could serve the Gospel.

When Paul was arrested for his preaching because of complaints filed by Thekla's fiancé, Thekla bribed the jail guards with her jewelry to let her into Paul's cell to talk with him further. After an extensive search of the city, she was discovered. Somehow Paul was set free, but the governor wished to deter other young women who might be smitten with Paul's preaching. Thekla was put on trial for shaming her fiancé and sentenced to be burned at the stake. A deluge of rain extinguished the fire and Thekla also was set free. She immediately left Iconium in pursuit of Paul. Here the ancient story grows even more interesting.

It turns out Paul was not particularly keen on having Thekla following him around. While he was happy to discover her alive, he tells her to wait on baptism and discourages her from going with him any further. When she persists in going with him to Antioch, one of the magistrates of the city falls in love with her and attempts to ask for her hand from Paul. Paul denies that he even knows her. The magistrate then makes further advances that she publicly rebuffs. And, like a bad dream that keeps repeating, Thekla is once again sent to the governor and condemned to death. This time beasts are let into the arena, but they refuse to eat her.

Now Thekla has had enough. If no one will baptize her after two near-martyrdom experiences . . . well, she will just have to do it herself. "In the name of Jesus Christ," she says, diving into a tank of water, "I baptize myself." The power of her splash instantly kills all the seals in the tank.

One last time, the executioners try to do away with her, tying her between bulls, but the cords that hold her deteriorate in flame. They turn to ash at her feet. The last line of the episode reads, "She was as one not bound."

The line aptly describes the remainder of Thekla's life. Leaving Antioch, she tracks Paul down in the town of Myra. "The Acts of Paul and Thekla" reads, "It was no small surprise to Paul when he saw her . . . for he

imagined some fresh trial was coming upon them."
But Thekla was not there to involve Paul in any further
mishaps, nor even to seek his guidance. She had come
to share the story of how she found her own voice in a
powerful way in the arena and how God had assisted
her in trial. She wanted to bring him money from the
community in Antioch so he could continue his mission
and to let him know she was going back to Iconium
with the implication that she would preach the Gospel
there. Paul replied to her, "Go, and teach the word of
the Lord."

Thekla is alleged to have lived to the age of ninety.
In the Orthodox Church, she is referred to as "Pro-
tomartyr and Equal to the Apostles." Her feast is cele-
brated each year at the end of September.

For Reflection *and* Prayer

1.   What have you experienced as the costs of speak-
     ing up in your own life? What have you experi-
     enced as the costs of not speaking up? Are they
     similar or different?

2.   In asserting your own point of view in a conversa-
     tion, do you lean in the direction of directly stating
     what you see and prefer or do you lean toward
     more mitigated forms of speech? Where did you
     learn your own speech patterns?

3. When you look at the conversations you have found most difficult in the last couple of years, has status played a complicating role? If so, how?

4. What inspiration do you draw from the life of Thekla regarding the challenge of "speaking up" in your own life?

Throughout all of history, O God,
you have expressed concern for the voiceless,
demanding that their concerns have a place at the
      table
and that their needs are not ignored.
Through your prophets you rattled the halls of
      power
and in Jesus showed us how to welcome the
      timid and the outcast.
Open my lips, O God, that I might speak fearlessly
      the truth
as best I am able to see it.
Open my ears, O God, that I might receive the
      truth when it comes in whispers from those
      whose voices I unwittingly dismiss.
Amen.

7. Know and Steady Thyself

For me to be a saint means to be myself.
Therefore the problem of sanctity and salvation is in fact the problem of finding out
who I am and of discovering my true self.

—Thomas Merton

Let me tell you a few things I know about myself. I am
hardworking: I regularly put in ten- to twelve-hour
days, and I have few leisure skills. I am, for the most
part, organized: I answer e-mails in a timely manner;
my filing system is orderly. I am fairly intelligent: I read
things; I can follow arguments. I had to get my first
pair of trifocals recently, and my son told me I looked
like a dorky professor. This does not bother me. I *am* a
dorky professor.

But let me tell you a few things that do bother
me: people who do not answer my e-mails, cluttered
houses and weedy gardens, chores others promised to
do that don't get done, and inane comments made at
committee meetings that reveal someone has not read
last month's minutes. I am apt to take note of these
"flaws" more than others and file them away in my

memory. But, I should say, these things don't keep me up at night.

Let me tell you what *would* keep me stewing in the middle of the night: the slightest insinuation that I am not pulling my weight on a project or that my thinking was scattered or a report not thorough. Likewise, I will be kept awake when, at the end of a semester, students say they did not get timely or substantive feedback on their assignments or when I am asked why I decided to hire someone to help with the yard rather than just do it myself.

There is a thread here, isn't there? One you could probably trace in the weave of your own life as well: different people find different *behaviors* problematic, but when we do find them problematic, it is because those behaviors go against our treasured values—our sense of what keeps the earth spinning rightly on its axis. Furthermore, different people find different *conversations* troublesome, but when we do find them troublesome, it is because those conversations somehow insinuate that we ourselves are not living up to the values we most treasure—that we are somehow not entirely the persons we believe ourselves to be.

Thus far, while naming habits we want to practice in the midst of conflict, we've also been subtly compiling a list of the most common reasons people give for why they detest being involved in conflict in the first place: conflict tangles our thought patterns, toys with our emotions, inflicts relational costs, confuses what we know, and makes it hard to listen. As we cross the midpoint in this text, it makes sense to pause for a moment and identify a single, haunting question running through all of these given reasons: "And what would that say about me?"

What would it say about me if I "lose it" trying to talk about this? What would it say about me if I really did hurt someone? What would it say about me if the way I'm looking at this isn't the only way to see it? What would it say about me if what the other person *is saying* about me is even partially true? The list could go on.

Ultimately, what makes conflict difficult is that it gives us information *about* ourselves that is tough to take in. It may be explicit. Or it may be implicit. But either way, it rocks our sense of self. The only thing that can transform conflict into a spiritual journey—a way of living our discipleship fully—is if we are open to having a conversation *within* ourselves concerning what the conflict implies *about* ourselves.

Noverim Me, Noverim Te

The great early bishop of the Church, Augustine of Hippo—whom we met in chapter 5—was known to have a favorite prayer that appeared frequently in his writing, almost like a mantra: "*Noverim me; noverim te.* May I know who I am; may I know who You are."[1] In Augustine's mind, the two parts of this prayer were not distinct petitions but deeply intertwined. If God was truth, Augustine couldn't know himself without knowing God, but he also couldn't know God without knowing himself. Maturing in the spiritual life required mature self-knowledge.

But Augustine also knew acquiring such knowledge was hard. Part of the difficulty lay in the nature of the task: in the words of the zen koan, "Can the eye see itself?" But part of the difficulty lay in the nature of sin. The human mind has a particular propensity, Augustine believed, toward deluding itself—to think it is loving and pursuing good when, as we talked about in chapter 4, really it is not.

Augustine spoke of two ways that God works in our lives to help us know ourselves as we really are: *foris*—the "exterior admonitions" that God speaks to us through the circumstances and people we meet in life—and *intus*—the "interior" space deep within each person where God dwells and nurtures understanding. In Augustine's understanding, *foris* is often experienced as a harsh teacher speaking to us uncomfortable words in order to wake us up, whereas *intus* is a gentle teacher that helps us to find meaning in what we hear and be at peace with it. The two work together.[2]

Although Augustine does not say so explicitly, conflict is a fertile field for "exterior admonition"— sometimes overtly in the others' words, many times just by what the situation itself seems to insinuate about us. In Augustine's framework, whether conflict helps us know ourselves more truly hinges on whether we believe God's voice might be trying to speak to us through the situation. But our learning and growth also hinges on whether we have the capacity to get in touch with the gentle inner space where God can soothe and make sense of what feels abrasive and just plain wrong.

Many of us err in one direction or the other. When a situation feels admonishing, we deny it has anything to say to us whatsoever: "The problem isn't me." "It's not my fault." "He doesn't understand me or my intent." "They've got me all wrong." We are deaf to the voice of God present in the world. Or, swinging in the other direction, we find ourselves quaking before the blast: "I'm the problem." "It's all my fault." "I am a dreadful person." "I've been found out." We are deaf to the calming voice of God deep within. Again, as Augustine says, we must allow the voices to work in harmony with each other.

Welcoming the Voice of God from Without

Researchers Douglas Stone and Sheila Heen note that receiving feedback—in essence, any information about oneself—is tough because it lies at the intersection of two very basic human needs: the need to learn and to grow and the need to be accepted and loved exactly as we are now.[3] We like acquiring information and insight. Our minds are obviously wired for it. And looking back, most of us would say with pride that we are not the same people we were ten years ago. We like to see ourselves as maturing, growing wiser, and learning from the experiences of life. But, in the moment, Stone and Heen observe, "The very fact of feedback suggests that how we are is not quite okay. So we bristle: Why can't you accept me for who I am and how I am? Why are there always more adjustments, more upgrades? Why is it *so hard* for you to understand me?"[4]

Becoming defensive in the face of feedback, especially in the context of conflict, is a means of protecting our current selves—not inherently a bad thing—but at the cost of some potentially significant insight about how we might grow. We keep our sense of self intact but miss the opportunity to learn something new about ourselves or, at least, something new about how we are being perceived by the other. God may be trying to answer our prayer *noverim me* in that moment, and we block it out.

Stone and Heen are very careful to say that learning from feedback is not the same as simply "taking the feedback." Feedback can be mean-spirited and abusive. Embedded in conflict, it often arrives in the form of accusations and exaggerations, even caricatures. Rather it is a question of looking for diamonds in the rough— information that may be valuable to have about how we are perceived or how we are impacting others, even though we wouldn't necessarily interpret the situation the same way they do or arrive at the same conclusions about what needs to change.

The first step in looking for what may be of value in feedback is acknowledging that others have information about us that we simply do not have. It sounds odd to admit, even counterintuitive. There is so very much going on within each of us that *only* we are privy to. But at the same time, while we see the world through our eyes, we are not able to see what we look like through the world's eyes. When I stand before a group and start to talk, the only face in the room I cannot see is my own. The only voice I am not hearing accurately is my own. (I hear what I sound like inside my head, but I am always surprised to find out how much deeper my voice is on recordings.) I know how I *mean* to come across, but I have no idea how I *actually* come across—unless someone else "shows me to me."

A few years ago, we had a couple over to dinner on our back porch. It was a lovely dinner with rich conversation on lots of interesting topics. The visiting husband enjoys photography and throughout the night, he snapped pictures at the dinner, including some close-ups of each of the persons present. A week later, he graciously e-mailed copies of the wonderful pictures he took of my husband and son, and a horrible picture of me. I was clearly furious. My eyebrows were furrowed and forehead scrunched. My eyes looked like I wanted to shoot red laser beams from them to incinerate whomever I was staring at. "What on earth?" I thought. It was a very pleasant dinner; I don't remember being upset at any point during the evening. I certainly don't remember wishing death upon anyone.

I asked my husband, "What happened at this dinner? When did I look like this?"

"What are you talking about?" my husband replied. "You look like that all the time."

"What?!" I exclaimed.

"That's your listening face," he explained.

Turns out my expression of pastoral care and concern looks like I want to do you in. Who knew? Apparently everyone but me.

That's hard to take. I like to think of myself as a pretty good listener. I teach the stuff, for goodness' sake. But there it was, captured on film, and it suddenly made a whole lot of feedback make a whole lot of sense.

"You are pretty intense." "Lighten up. You are too serious." "I don't get why you are angry." "Stop judging me." This is all feedback that I've received before but never inquired about. Were they *all* trying to let me know about The Face?

With a photograph, all the evidence is before us. That's rare. Instead, most of the feedback we get from others consists of quick "tips," roundabout observations or—in times of conflict—frustrated complaints. It comes in the form of what Argyris would call "conclusions" or what Stone and Heen would call "labels."[5] Things like "You're so irresponsible" or "Geez, stop being so elitist" or "Why do you always have to be so serious?" These aren't the data itself—the observations they made about you. These are this person's interpretation of your words or actions. In order to simply understand what the other is trying to say—not to decide whether I think the label is right or wrong, true or false—I'm going to have to manage my own frustrated reaction and be daring enough to ask some questions:

- "You said that the way I handled the situation was irresponsible. That's hard to hear since I like to think of myself as uber-responsible. So I want to understand better: What was it you saw that struck you as irresponsible?"

- "Can we back up for a moment? Say more about coming across as 'elitist.' Was there something I did or said that came across that way to you?"

Resist the impulse to defend yourself immediately and explain away the other's observation. A little further into the conversation, you may choose to share what your intent actually was. But for the moment, you are just collecting information—not to use against the other person but to know yourself. Or at least the self that others see.

To know oneself truthfully requires cultivating a habit of asking—indeed, a habit of not only being open to feedback when it naturally arises but also a habit of seeking it, which sometimes means being willing to revisit conflicts even after the heat has dissipated.

- "You said something the other day that has stuck with me—that I was 'selfish.' I am not bringing this up to restart an argument. I've just been thinking about it more and wondered what you meant by it."

- "When you said last week that I 'wasn't listening to you again'—was that something you'd experienced before? Do you see this as a pattern for me?"

You will not agree with everything everyone says. You might not even agree with anything anyone says. Remember they are not giving you information about *you* but rather information about how you are being *perceived* or *experienced* by them. Some of it will be random and novel and will never find a place in the narrative you tell to yourself about yourself. But if it hits a nerve—if it makes you jump like the rubber hammer "pinging" at a reflex—it is worth just paying attention to, even if you don't know why right away.

Jody Scheier is one of the most remarkable psychologists I've ever witnessed in action. She will sometimes have clients role play an argument that they are having a particularly difficult time working through in real life. In the midst of the role play, she walks around to the back of the client and lays her hand on his shoulder. She then speaks, as if from inside the recesses of his mind, "This has never happened to me before. No one has ever said anything like this to me before."

Almost every time, the person will startle and go quiet. For a moment, it is a scene straight from Augustine's *Confessions*, where he says:

> I venture over the spacious structures of memory, where treasures are stored. . . . Some things, summoned, are instantly delivered up, though others require a longer search, to be drawn from recesses less penetrable. And, all the while, jumbled memories flirt out on their own, interrupting the search for what we want, pestering: 'Wasn't it us you were seeking?' My heart strenuously waves these things off from my memory's gaze until the dim thing sought arrives at last, fresh from depths.[6]

There is a moment of awakening. Of course it had happened before. Sometimes many times before. With other people at other times, but the same pattern of interaction, the same feedback. There was something here worth attending to. The voice of God is whispering. We just need to lean in to hear.

Welcoming the Voice of God from Within

When the challenging words of others strike a nerve, when we spot a pattern for the first time or—worse yet—see an old pattern reemerging for the twelfth time, it is not a pleasant sensation. Instead of adamantly proclaiming, "It's not true!" we begin to wonder, "What if it is all true?" We flip from "defensiveness" to "defenselessness." And just as defensiveness has its perils, defenselessness does as well. It evokes shame. In the words of pastoral theologian Brad Binau,

> Shame is a painful self-consciousness that we are somehow *less* than what we want to be or think we should be. It is a feeling of being "wrong"— not simply that we have *done* something wrong (that is more the feeling of guilt)—but a feeling that our very *being* is somehow "wrong." And in our "wrongness" we feel exposed, vulnerable, and unlovable.[7]

The feedback begins to take on a depressingly "timeless" quality in the sense that what we've just learned about ourselves in *this* present moment in *this* relationship suddenly balloons in our mind to include *all* of our relationships—current, past, and future. I've always been this way. I am this way now. I will always be this way. Stone and Heen refer to this propensity to inflate the meaning of feedback as "Google bias." It is as if someone typed "Ann is lazy" into our emotional search engine and a barrage of memories flood our mind.[8] It can be horrifying. Painful. Paralyzing.

Everyone has moments where they feel total *yuck* about what just happened and about themselves. As mentioned in chapter 5, each of us has a unique feeling fingerprint. So how much "yuck" we feel and how long it lasts before we feel steady on our feet again is going to vary widely. But, for starters, it helps to know one's own patterns.

When I feel horrible about something, it takes twenty-four hours before I can think straight and stop obsessing about it during daylight hours; seventy-two hours before I stop obsessing between 2 and 4 a.m.; and a week before I have incorporated what happened into the story line of my life and allowed it to find its right place in proportion to everything else I tell myself about myself. This pattern isn't true always and everywhere. But it is predictable enough that when things happen, I can send my quaking innards a message to help quell the Google bias: "You are going to feel miserable for the next twenty-four hours. In a week, you will be okay." And that alone helps.

But what I am really counting on is that within the next twenty-four hours, the voice of God that dwells deep within is going to begin to go to work. Augustine speaks of this voice as *interior intimo meo*—"deeper in me than I am in me." He names it as the one who knows us better than we know ourselves: "*intus eras et ego foris*"—"You were inside me, I outside me."[9] And, from age to age, this voice has said pretty much the same thing: "I love you, I will not leave you, and we can work with this."

The voice of God from without arrives in an ever-dizzying array of unexpected forms. The voice of God from within arises in silence, but it is often stirred into action by familiar faces—those of our friends. To return to Augustine: "*Nemo nisi per amicatiam cognoscitur*"—"No one learns except by friendship."[10]

The importance of friendship was a frequent theme in Augustine's writing, as it has been throughout Christian writing on spirituality and moral development. In its original context, Augustine's favored phrase implied that you cannot really know a person (or any subject matter) unless you are well disposed toward it, have affection for it, and approach it as a friend. But for Augustine, surely the reverse was also true: you yourself can't grow and learn unless you've got people out there who are well disposed and affectionate toward you. From ancient times, friendship has been regarded as a "school of virtue"—a place where we can become better people precisely because it is a place we can feel safe to fail and make mistakes and still know ourselves as loved.

Good friends help to correct the Google bias by typing other messages into our search engine so that we aren't simply flooded with memories of "Ann is lazy" but also read the entries tagged "Ann is productive," "Ann makes a contribution," "Ann is useful to have around." Friends help us to balance the upsetting feedback we just heard with other data that fills out a more realistic sense of self.

Our best friends can do even more, if we let them. Like the divine Good Shepherd, the best friends simply know and call us by name and not by adjectives. Into the search engine, they just type "Ann" and remain alongside us as we watch the fuller picture come to light. A picture that includes both virtue and vice, the normal and the quirky. They can help us to see our complexity, and they can model for us the radical acceptance of God. The key phrase is "if we let them." If friendship is to function truly as a school of virtue, we'll need to ask those we trust to help us make sense of the feedback we receive—not just to tell us where it was partially wrong but where it might be partially right. We must allow them to mirror the voice of God in saying, "I love you, I will not leave you, and we can work with this."

I suspect the clearer we are able to hear the voice of unconditional love and acceptance in our lives, the easier it will be to winnow what is useful from the feedback and let go of the rest. The more distant we feel from that voice, the harder it will be to heal and the harder it will be in the future not to tilt in the direction of self-protective defensiveness.

A Final Thought

Remember that everything said in this chapter goes two ways. Just as our own sense of self is often threatened in situations of conflict, so is the other party's. When other people overreact, what you have just said has probably touched a sensitive place in their own identities. It may remind them of something that happened in their pasts. It may touch upon something that they value about themselves. Rather than react back, recognize you've stumbled across something close to another person's core and that is a sacred space. It is not unlike stumbling upon a wild animal in the forest. Tread carefully.

You might decide to back away and be respectful of that space—especially if it is not a relationship that is especially close or long-lasting. Perhaps you've stepped into territory you wish to leave in God's hands. If it *is* a close or long-standing relationship, however, you might decide to stay in this sacred space so as to understand better what is important for the other person, far beyond the immediate disagreement. But remember, in the words of writer Parker Palmer, "The soul is shy. . . . If we want to see a wild animal, the last thing we should do is go crashing through the woods yelling for it to come out."[11]

The most successful language in these moments is not demanding but observational and invitational:

- "It seems like what I just said has hit a nerve. Do you want to say more about that?"

- "This seems important to you at a very deep level."

When followed by silence, such phrases give the other the freedom to say more. Or not. Palmer continues:

> If we will walk quietly into the woods [and] sit patiently at the base of a tree, the wild creature we seek might put in an appearance. We may see it only briefly and only out of the corner of an

eye—but the sight is a gift we will always treasure as an end in itself.[12]

No one learns except by friendship.

Companions for the Journey:
Oscar Romero and Rutilio Grande

It was an unlikely friendship: Oscar Romero was shy and bookish, nervous to rock the boat and anxious to avoid the spotlight. Rutilio Grande was outspoken and creative, fearless and passionate. But they became friends with one another while teaching at the diocesan major seminary in El Salvador in the 1960s. Grande would soon move on to parish ministry among the *campesinos* of Aguilares. He became a vocal critic of government policies that preserved the wealth of the fourteen land-owning families in the country while keeping those without access to land in ongoing poverty. Romero would soon pursue the path of ecclesial administration—becoming auxiliary bishop of San Salvador in 1970 and then bishop of the rural diocese of Santiago de María in 1974.

Upon hearing of Romero's appointment as archbishop of San Salvador in 1977, Grande's Jesuit community grumbled with disappointment. The situation in El Salvador was worsening, and Romero seemed adverse to any sort of confrontation. All of his actions to this point indicated a desire to simply preserve the status quo and squelch movements within the Church advocating for social change. A member of Grande's community later remembered, "I didn't like him. He was an insignificant being, a shadow that went by clinging to the walls."[13] Grande, however, saw more in Romero—perhaps more than Romero himself.

Rather than backing away, Grande drew near to Romero, sticking with him through the criticism but also seeking to expose him to the realities of the countryside, encouraging him to take the feedback from brother priests to get out among the *campesinos*. He was fond of saying, "the Gospel must grow little feet" if Jesus was not to remain a distant figure in the clouds.[14] Shortly before Romero's installation as archbishop, Grande gave his most challenging homily yet—sometimes referred to as the "Apopa Sermon" after the city in which he delivered it.

> I am very much afraid that soon the Bible and the Gospel will not be able to enter at our borders. . . . If Jesus of Nazareth returned, coming down from Chalatenango to San Salvador, I dare say he would not arrive . . . even to Apopa; they would arrest him for being a subversive and would crucify him again.[15]

Preaching like this triggered only anxiety in Romero. As another member of Grande's community recalled, "He couldn't just take a stand and move on it.

. . . The man would get so nervous, he'd develop a tick. The corner of his lip would start trembling. It would shake and shake, and he couldn't control it."[16] Nevertheless, Romero remained open to Grande's challenge and invited him into his inner circle. He asked Grande to serve as the master of ceremonies at his installation celebration on February 22.

Three weeks later, on March 12, 1977, Rutilio Grande and two *campesinos* were gunned down by government forces while driving from Aguilares to the nearby town of El Paisnal. One of the *campesinos*, a seventy-two-year-old man named Manuel Solorzano, had apparently tried to cover the priest with his own body to protect him from the rain of bullets but could not.

Upon hearing the news, something within Romero snapped. In the words of one writer, "The silencing of Rutilio broke the silence of Romero."[17] Two days later, Romero preached Grande's funeral Mass: "I considered [him] a brother and at important moments in my life, he was very close to me and I will never forget his gestures of friendship," he said.[18] Immediately afterward, Romero issued an announcement that he would not appear at any official government functions again until there had been an investigation of the killings. Furthermore, he cancelled all Masses for the following Sunday, save one to be concelebrated by all of the priests in the diocese in the cathedral in San Salvador. More than one hundred thousand people converged upon the city's center. One of his fellow concelebrants recorded this memory:

> As the Mass began, I noted that Monseñor Romero was sweating, pale and nervous. And when he began the homily, it seemed slow to me . . . as if he was reluctant to go through the door of history that God was opening up for him. But after about five minutes, I felt the Holy Spirit descend up on him.[19]

On that day, Romero began to speak with the passion and bravery of Grande. He began to take up the cause of the *campesinos* and condemn government violence against them. Romero was finally ready and able to see what before he had earlier been resistant to seeing in his country and in himself. Although he had been installed several weeks earlier, he would later speak of that day, March 20, as the day when he truly became bishop of the people of San Salvador.

Romero's outspoken preaching and prophetic action continued, resulting in his own death by government-sanctioned gunfire only three years later on March 24, 1980.

For Reflection and Prayer

1. What adjectives would you use to describe your truest self? When you look at the situations that most provoke you, do you resonate with the

claim that somehow they challenge your sense of identity?

2. When in a difficult conversation, do you see yourself naturally tilting more in the direction of "defensiveness" or "defenselessness"? What kinds of things have helped you to recover your sense of balance?

3. What clues indicate to you that you've said or done something that threatened a person's core identity? What have you found to work best in those situations?

4. What insights does the friendship of Rutilio Grande and Oscar Romero offer as you reflect on your own struggles to grow as a person in the context of friendship?

N*overim te; noverim me*, O Lord.

I make this age-old prayer my own.

May I know who I am; may I know who you are.

But, all I ask is this: be gentle. I want to grow. I
    want to learn.

I want to know myself truthfully.

But, it is a lot to take in, maybe more than I am
    prepared to swallow today.

So as I strive to open myself to the challenging
    conversations of life,

I ask you to speak words of comfort in my ear.

I need to know you love me; you will not leave
    me;

and you will help me make sense of what I am
    hearing.

Noverim te; noverim me.

Amen.

8. Pray to Forgive

Then Peter came and said to him, "Lord, if another member of the church sins against me, how often should I forgive? As many as seven times?" Jesus said to him, "Not seven times, but, I tell you, seventy-seven times."

—Matthew 18:21–22

Let's imagine for a moment that you've done all of the things we've been talking about in this book. You've listened. You kind of understand where the other is coming from and what motivated him or her to do what was done. You still don't agree it was the right thing to do, and you've spoken up about that. You've shared the impact on you and how you feel. In fact, maybe you've even had this conversation a couple of times now. You're not really satisfied with the outcome of all this talk. Maybe you're still not feeling heard. Maybe you still don't think the other person gets it. Maybe you long for an apology and it has not been forthcoming. And a voice suggests, "Let it go." Sometimes the voice arises from within. Sometimes it comes from a trusted friend who has been hearing of your troubles for a while. Many times it is the offending party making the recommendation and in a not-so-sympathetic manner: "Are you ever just going to let this drop?" In this chapter, I am going to walk out on very thin ice to broach the topic of forgiveness.

On one hand, to talk about forgiveness should hardly seem dicey at all. There are innumerable medical studies that validate its health benefits. People who demonstrate a capacity to forgive report lower incidences of depression and chronic stress-related illnesses. They are at a reduced risk for high blood pressure and heart attacks, insomnia, migraines, ulcers, and even cancer.[1] Who wouldn't advocate forgiveness as a practice?

Furthermore, this is a book for Christians, and isn't forgiveness part of the bedrock of the Christian faith? How can I say forgiveness is a touchy topic when there exist any number of scriptural passages in which Jesus teaches about forgiveness, tells stories about forgiveness, or articulates forgiveness himself? Even from the cross, he preaches on this topic. What more is there to say on the matter? Just do it. Isn't that what we hear from the pulpit on a regular basis?

It is not so simple, is it?

We all know people who we suspect would benefit tremendously from the capacity to let things go. A few years ago, the professional-negotiation community was abuzz when one of its own—a respected scholar who taught the subject at a top-notch business school—was outed in the media for threatening legal action against the immigrant owner of a small Chinese restaurant over a four-dollar discrepancy in his bill. Clearly the restaurant owner had made a mistake, but—really? As dozens of commenters asked, "Is this the battle hill you want to die on?"

When the grievance is our own, however, it never feels so clear. And for others to say—even hint—that it is time to let go feels demeaning, insulting, and like adding salt to the wound. The recommendation to move on seems to invalidate the hurt we've experienced. It suggests the erasure of a memory that we find valuable, if only to protect ourselves against the same sort of thing happening again. Sure, forgiveness is a good, but there are other goods like justice and dignity and truth that also need to be affirmed. Should forgiveness trump those? Never mind the hardest question of all: let's just say I decide I *will* forgive . . . *and then I can't*. In addition to all that has happened to me, now *I* am the one at fault for not being able to "get over it"? Where's the justice in that?

For every article that has been written on the benefits of forgiveness there are two letters to the editor calling for justice and accountability. For every sermon that has been preached on letting bygones be bygones, there is someone in the pew who feels victimized anew.

A robust practice of Christian conflict needs to be undergirded by a healthy theology of forgiveness.

Resourcing the Christian Tradition

As with the topic of truth, entire libraries could be filled trying to capture all that the Christian tradition has to say on the topic of forgiveness, not to mention justice and dignity. Perhaps the first and most important point to make is that, from the tradition's point of view, we don't need to lodge ourselves in one of these libraries to the exclusion of the others. Frameworks that pit forgiveness against a concern for justice, dignity, or truth are working out of an unnecessarily weak definition of forgiveness.

Jesus's teachings on forgiveness—the roots of the Christian tradition on the topic—make the most sense when understood within their original historical context. Anthropologists describe first-century Mediterranean culture as marked by an "honor-and-shame" worldview.[2] In such a context, "honor" or "saving face" was associated with refusal to forgive offenses against oneself or one's family. Holding on to the offense was perceived as a form of power, a way to hold the wrongdoer in one's debt. In contrast, forgiveness was perceived as a weakness, an inability to protect one's own honor, and a lack of loyalty to one's family.

Jesus's preaching directly confronts these cultural assumptions. He proclaims forgiveness not as a weakness but rather as a strength. It is a power that in its origins belongs only to God—a power that God exercises as Creator to always be making of creation something new. Rather than being locked into cycles of ill-will and impasse, God exerts this divine capacity to liberate a situation that feels stuck. It is one of God's greatest powers, one that Jesus fully embraced for himself. And one that he wanted to share with us: in the upper room on the night of his resurrection, he breathed on his disciples the same divine spirit that had animated his life and gave them this power. "If you forgive the sins of any, they are forgiven them" (Jn 20:23).

From God's point of view, for whom is the power of forgiveness meant as a gift? It is for the "little ones of the earth"—the ones who feel powerless and taken advantage of, the ones who are suffering the negative impact of another's action, the ones who have experienced injury. Pastoral counselor Marie Fortune writes,

> Any benefit that it [forgiveness] brings to offenders is a bonus. . . . Forgiveness is God's gift, for the purpose of healing, to those who have been harmed. Accountability is God's gift to those who have harmed another for the purpose of repentance."[3]

What does it mean to say that forgiveness is primarily a gift *from* God *to* the injured? This is a difficult concept to understand in part because it is so very different than our typical view of forgiveness, which is that of a gift the injured is expected to offer the offender. But those like Fortune who work with people who have suffered profound injury recognize that human memory works at several different levels. There was the original injuring event, which is what it is, but each time we remember that event, it stirs up hurt again and again. Forgiveness does not undo the original event. What it changes is how we remember it so that the original event does not keep hurting us and our relationships with others each time we remember it. "In forgiveness we do not forget," emphasizes theologian Robert Schreiter. "We remember in a different way." Schreiter goes on to say,

> Forgiveness means that the balance of power has passed from the traumatic event to the victim. The victim chooses the direction of the future and does not follow the trajectory laid out by the traumatic event.[4]

Schreiter illustrates his point by referencing the wounds of the resurrected Jesus. When Jesus rose from the dead, his body was clearly transformed—no one was able to recognize him at first glance. But even on his resurrected body, he still carried the wounds of his crucifixion. Resurrection doesn't "fix" or erase the crucifixion. It happened, but it isn't going to determine Jesus's future.[5] To quote the comedian Lily Tomlin, "Forgiveness is letting go of every hope for a better past." Not a better present or a better future, but freedom from constantly being constrained by the past. We can chart another course.

Anglican Archbishop Desmond Tutu, who oversaw the Truth and Reconciliation Commission in South Africa, notes that the "new course" is never a restoration of the old relationship but rather a renewal of the relationship, or a release. "We do not make a carbon copy of the relationship we had before the hurt or insult," says Tutu. "Renewing a relationship is a creative act. . . . We create a new relationship out of our suffering, one that is often stronger for what we have experienced together."[6] He goes on to explain, "Releasing a relationship [is choosing] to not have someone in your life any longer, but you have released the relationship only when you have truly chosen that path without wishing that person ill."[7]

In their ministries, Schreiter, Fortune, and Tutu all work with persons who have suffered physical, mental, and sexual abuse, and even torture. In those settings, renewal of any type of ongoing personal relationship between the injured and the offender would be extremely rare and generally ill-advised. In those very unlikely circumstances where some sort of renewal of the relationship has taken place, it is because the act of forgiveness was also accompanied by sincere and tangible signs of repentance by the offending party.[8] Not all relationships can be renewed, but even in the absence of apology, forgiveness is still possible as a gift from God to allow the aggrieved to experience freedom.

As with all good gifts, sometimes we find ourselves lacking the amount needed in a particular situation, in which case we are left in the position of asking and waiting. Forgiveness is not something that we can perform on demand out of our own store of goodwill but only out of God's abundance. There may be occasions in our lives where the gravity of the offense is such that we don't find it within our current capacity to forgive. In those situations where we find ourselves depleted, we can place things back in the hands of God, drawing on the scriptural examples of Jesus on the cross and Stephen in the book of Acts, neither of whom spoke of forgiving their executioners themselves in the midst of their suffering but rather called on God to do what they could not.[9]

I sometimes wonder when Jesus told Peter that he'd need to forgive seventy-seven times whether he was speaking of seventy-seven different offenses committed by one party or whether he was referring to the fact that sometimes just one event might require us to forgive seventy-seven times. One blessed morning we find that we are able to let anger and hurt go, but the next morning it is back, and we must ask for the gift to be able to forgive yet again. Like manna in the desert, it is a gift that often comes in small doses and keeps us dependent on God's goodness.

With that in mind, the wisdom from tradition's storehouse seems to be, "Ask and ask repeatedly." Don't demand from yourself the ability to forgive if it is not there yet, and don't feel compelled to say, "I forgive" if it doesn't feel truthful. But ask for the gift to be given and be willing to participate in the gift of forgiveness should God choose to move within you.

Tutu captures something of the essence of the Christian tradition's stance toward the gift when he reflects:

> I am not yet ready for the journey
> I am not yet interested in the path
> I am at the prayer before the prayer of forgive
> ness
> Grant me the will to want to forgive
> Grant it to me not yet but soon.[10]

Preparing to Receive the Gift

God is often not particularly stingy when we ask for something (especially when we ask repeatedly and when it is something God clearly likes giving). So, beware—when you ask for the gift of forgiveness you should probably prepare yourself for the request to be answered.

There are a number of valuable exercises one can do to ready for the gift of forgiveness, many of which are helpfully described at length in both online and written resources.[11] They commonly include talking aloud about what has happened with a trusted friend or trained counselor, journaling or letter writing, meditation, and rituals of letting go. Many of the resources on forgiveness seem to presume events of deep injury rather than the run-of-the-mill conflicts faced in daily life. But that is not to say that the same types of practices are not helpful in ordinary life as well.

In daily life, the gift of forgiveness is often less associated with particular events and more associated with the development of an attitude—a way of being in relationship that doesn't look for offense and doesn't cling to hurts. Forgiveness should never be associated with dishonesty—in essence, sweeping things under the rug, saying "it's okay" when it's not—but rather a broad sense of truth that is able to see the weight of a particular offense in the bigger scheme of things. One of the most memorable sermons I ever heard was crafted around the statement, "Sometimes it is better to belong than be right." Now obviously that is not true always and everywhere, but when we are arguing over who lost the remote, whether the mailing went out on time, or the four-dollar overcharge on the Chinese-food bill, there is a great deal of wisdom in that sentiment. Through forgiveness, we may choose to release our unhealthy relationships, but without forgiveness, we will not be able to maintain or renew even our healthy ones.

In these day-to-day scenarios, to even speak of the gift of forgiveness aloud can feel overdramatic. When I say to my husband that I "forgive" him for painting the kitchen bright yellow while I was out of town, he thinks I have chosen the wrong verb. He still thinks he has done me a favor and can't fathom why I am offended (even though I was very explicit about the fact I didn't *want* the kitchen painted yellow . . . and have stated this multiple times now . . . over the course of ten years). He still doesn't think *forgiveness* is the right framework for me to be operating in, but in the long run, it is not a question of whether I am right to feel wronged or not. I do feel wronged. And, as the one who feels wronged, *I* still need the power of forgiveness in my life in order to keep the relationship a healthy one. Whether the decision to let something go is articulated aloud (which seems important in incidents of significant injury) or just whispered in my own heart (which often seems to make more sense in the ordinary stuff), being able to say "I forgive you" is still key to renewing a life lived in communion with others. "The words are so small," says Tutu, "but there is a universe hidden in them."[12]

Companion for the Journey: **Corrie ten Boom**

For more than a hundred years, Corrie ten Boom's family had owned a watch-making shop on Barteljoris-straat in the Netherlands' city of Haarlem. Although they were devout Dutch Reformed Christians, they'd long enjoyed a close relationship with their Jewish neighbors—often partaking in Sabbath celebrations and annual feasts while also hosting weekly prayer meetings for peace in Jerusalem.

When Germany invaded the Netherlands in 1940, the ten Booms did not abandon their friendships within the Jewish community but rather deepened them. Corrie's brother, Willem, a Dutch Reformed minister, used the nursing home he administered to lodge Jews fleeing Germany. Corrie, her sister Betsie, and their father Caspar, turned their home above the family store into a hiding place both for Jews and members of the Dutch resistance. In the early 1940s, they generally had six to seven additional persons living with them and created a special secret chamber behind a false wall in Corrie's bedroom should the property be searched. Corrie also worked to establish a network of additional homes where Jews could hide within the city.

On February 28, 1944, a man came to the shop under the guise of seeking Corrie's assistance when in reality he was an informant. Later that day, the ten Boom home was raided, and although the lodgers were able to make it into the secret chamber undiscovered, Corrie and her family were arrested. Eighty-two-year-old Caspar died after only ten days of imprisonment. Corrie and Betsie were sent to three different prisons over the course of the next ten months, the last being Ravensbrück, the notorious women's concentration camp near Berlin.

Upon arriving at the camp, the women were forced to strip and walk before the prison guards under bright lights. Corrie found the treatment humiliating and cruel, and her anger toward the Germans continued to build. Betsie, even as her health deteriorated, continued to nudge Corrie in the direction of forgiveness.

Before her death in mid-December, Betsie's urged Corrie, "[We] must tell [others] what we have learned here: We must tell them that there is no pit so deep that He is not deeper still."[13]

Shortly after Betsie's death, Corrie was taken aside in the prison and mysteriously handed a one-word card reading "Released." By the time the clerical error had been discovered, Corrie had already been boarded upon a train to Berlin. It was January 1, 1945. Days later all of the other women at Ravensbrück in Corrie's age bracket were sent to the gas chambers.

Corrie made her way back to Haarlem to reunite with remaining family members and work in the family shop. But as the war came to a close, Betsie's witness of forgiveness echoed in her mind. By May of that year, Corrie had rented a house to serve as a home for persons with disabilities and former prisoners of concentration camps. Soon the home also began to welcome Dutch citizens who had worked with the German authorities during the war and were now being ostracized within their home communities. By June she had written an account of her experiences. Her testimony, especially her emphasis on forgiveness, touched many deeply.

Within a year, Corrie was speaking about the importance of forgiveness in a variety of settings across Western Europe and the United States. Her convictions were tested, however, at a church in Munich in 1947 when, as she spoke, she spotted sitting in a pew one of the guards from the Ravensbrück prison. "It came back with a rush," she says, "the huge room with its harsh overhead lights; the pathetic piles of dresses and shoes in the center of the floor; the shame of walking naked past this man."[14]

Afterward, the man approached her. He did not remember her but acknowledged he'd been a guard at Ravensbrück. He held out his hand and asked for her forgiveness. Corrie recalls:

> And I, who had spoken so glibly of forgiveness, fumbled in my pocketbook rather than take that hand. . . . I stood there with the coldness clutching my heart. But forgiveness is not an emotion—I knew that. Forgiveness is an act of the will, and the will can function regardless of the temperature of the heart. . . . "Help!" I prayed silently. "I can lift my hand. I can do that much. You supply the feeling."
>
> And so woodenly, mechanically, I thrust my hand into the one stretched out to me. And as I did, an incredible thing took place. The current started in my shoulder, raced down my arm, sprang into our joined hands. And then this healing warmth seemed to flood my whole being, bringing tears to my eyes.
>
> "I forgive you, brother!" I cried.[15]

Corrie later acknowledged that such forgiveness was not a one-time act. Often, after forgiving, the anger would resurface and she would have to forgive again.

She likened it to the ringing of a bell that even after you had let go of the rope would continue to "dong," though gradually more quietly, until finally the sound would cease.[16]

Corrie spent the next thirty years speaking about forgiveness in sixty countries worldwide until her death at the age of ninety-one.

For Reflection *and* Prayer

1. What are your own convictions about forgiveness? Do you see it as always possible? As wise? Are there limits that you would place on the practice?

2. Why do you think this chapter is called "Pray to Forgive" rather than "Forgive"? What role do you see for God in the process of forgiveness?

3. Can you think of a time in your own life when forgiveness seemed unlikely and suddenly it was possible? What helped to move you into a space of forgiveness?

4. What insight from the life of Corrie ten Boom would you want to take with you as you reflect on the practice of forgiveness in your own life?

I have many memories, O Lord—both positive
    and painful.
These memories have helped me to grow in
    wisdom
and I don't want to let go of any of them,
lest I be forced to learn life's hard-won lessons
    over and over again.
But sometimes, my God, remembering stings,
and although the memory is from long ago,
it continues to hurt me anew each time it comes
    to mind.
And I should like to be free.
So I ask what seems impossible:
that I should be able to keep the wisdom but be
    released of the pain.
I turn to you because you are the only one
who could make such a crazy request real.
Grant me the gift of forgiveness.
Amen.

9. Repent

> Zacchaeus stood there and said to the Lord, "Look, half of my possessions, Lord, I will give to the poor; and if I have defrauded anyone of anything, I will pay back four times as much." Then Jesus said to him, "Today salvation has come to this house."
>
> —Luke 19:8–9

Wow—so when is the last time you saw the word "repent" scrawled across the top of a page? Unless you are a devotee of John the Baptist or Puritan literature, it has probably been a while. Maybe during Advent or Lent the term makes an appearance or two, in a sermon or homily or in the pastor's weekly bulletin column, but in our wider culture the word seems antiquated, a relic from another era. It sounds harsh and confrontational and calls to mind images of fire and brimstone. Perhaps it seems out of step with the tone of rest of this book.

Within the wider Christian tradition, however, the possibility of repentance also arrives as gift. If out of goodness, God offers forgiveness as a gift to set free those who experience being wronged, it makes sense that out of that same goodness, God would also want to offer a gift to those who experience themselves *in* the wrong. It makes sense that God extends to them, too, a gift that they might find themselves freed of the endless cycle of revenge and tit-for-tat that holds human relationships hostage.

Marie Fortune, whom we met in chapter 8, names that gift "accountability"[1]—the gift of someone or something awakening within us the capacity to see ourselves and the impact of our actions more clearly than we had before. Like forgiveness, the awakening associated with accountability doesn't undo the original event but alters our relationship to it so that we now remember it in a different light. We see it more truthfully than we had before, and that awareness leads us to want and to work for a different sort of future— which is another way of saying, it leads us to *repent*.

Chances are that God wants the gift of accountability for us as much as forgiveness, but my suspicion is that accountability probably flourishes less within human relationships than forgiveness because we so rarely ask for it. As the poet Charles Williams notes, "Many promising reconciliations have broken down because while both parties come prepared to forgive, neither party comes prepared to be forgiven."[2] If it runs contrary to human instinct to forgive, it's even more contrary to our nature to think we've done something that requires forgiveness.

But much of what we've talked about in earlier chapters of this book, if embraced wholeheartedly, *is* about embracing the gift of accountability. Realizing that there is a difference between intent and impact and learning to ask about it explicitly in a tough conversation wakes us up to the fact that we have done harm, even if we didn't necessarily mean to. Asking further questions about challenging feedback we've received can open our eyes to a wider picture of self and how we are coming across to others. Although indirect, when we cultivate a practice of curiosity in conflict, we are opening ourselves to God's gift.

And if, in the course of your practice of conflict, you've stumbled upon a new degree of awareness—"Aaagh, I've had a role in this!" "I did another damage." "I blew it!"—the good news of the Christian tradition is that you don't need to remain stuck spinning in your own internal search engine of shame, and the relationship doesn't need to remain stuck there either. Alongside forgiveness, there is another way to unclog the relationship, and that is repentance.

On Saying "I'm Sorry"

Most models of the process of repentance begin with three simple words: "I am sorry." "Truth be told," says Desmond Tutu, "those three words often feel like the hardest words to say to another human being. Those three words can die in our mouths a hundred times before we say them."[3]

Several years ago, I was working with a group of women in a business-leadership seminar. "What do you do when you've made a decision that in retrospect you wish you hadn't?" one of them asked. "You say, 'I'm sorry,'" I replied. A rumble moved through the room. "The previous speaker told us that as women we should never apologize in the workplace," one stated. Now, the previous speaker was not there to explain herself further, but I suspect this message was communicated out of concern that women sometimes decrease their credibility as leaders by seeming apologetic for their very being. This certainly can be problematic. We never have to apologize for *who we are*. But throughout life, there *will* be times when we experience guilt for particular actions, even in the workplace, and it is equally problematic to say, "Never apologize." In doing so, we rob people of the most meaningful and effective way to "unstick" a relationship in impasse. Even studies from the legal world bear this out. As a single example, the University of Michigan Health System notes that since adopting a rapid-disclosure and apology program for medical errors in 2004, it has been able to decrease legal costs by 61 percent and per-case payments by 47 percent. The average time needed to reach a settlement has dropped from twenty months to six.[4]

At the same time, *how* we say "I am sorry" matters tremendously. There is nothing magic about the words themselves, and if said casually they can sometimes do more damage than good.

Literature on apology often draws a distinction between regret and remorse. Regret means that one is unhappy with the consequences of one's actions. The results were different than hoped, but under the same circumstances, the same action might be taken again. When the gate agents at the airport tell me that they regret my flight has been cancelled and that they are sorry for any inconvenience this causes, the sentiment is mildly appreciated, but I harbor no illusions that this will not happen again. Indeed, depending on the cause of the cancellation, I myself might choose to make such a call. The agents making the announcement do not see themselves as morally implicated in the action, and likely their greatest regret (at least it would be mine if I were a gate agent) is that they themselves have to now deal with 184 irate passengers. Such expressions of apology, observed seventeenth-century writer François de la Rochefoucauld, are often "not so much a concern and remorse for the harm we have done, as a fear of the harm we may have brought upon ourselves."[5]

Remorse, in contrast, realizes that there *was* a moral dimension to the offense, in that there was a *choice* involved and one that the person wishes he or she had made differently. It doesn't necessarily mean that one made the choice with full knowledge or freedom. One may not have anticipated bad outcomes. At the time, maybe it seemed like the best option. But one takes ownership of the choice and the consequences resulting from that choice. And, should a similar circumstance present itself again in the future, one is committed to taking another path. Remorse is a feeling one expresses only for one's own actions—no one else's.

A way to distinguish between remorse and regret is whether the phrase "I'm sorry" is followed by the phrase "that I" or "that you" (or variations thereof). "I'm sorry that I shared what was your private information with Britney at the coffee and doughnuts on Sunday" is remorse. "I'm sorry that you feel hurt" is regret. "I'm sorry I told that joke at the party" is remorse. "I'm sorry if you were offended" is regret. Regret is a perfectly fine sentiment for conveying sympathy: "I'm so sorry your grandpa is in the hospital—and right before the holidays." But only if one was not involved in the incident that landed him there. If you were the one who food-poisoned Grandpa, even if unwittingly, the comment will more likely magnify the grievance than diminish it.

If you are wanting to convey remorse rather than sympathy—in essence, if you are pursuing repentance rather than "good-neighborliness"—be very specific about which choices you made that you wish you had made otherwise. Take ownership for those choices and be clear about what you would do differently in the future.

- "I am really sorry that I've been leaving the hall in disarray after Bible study on Wednesday nights. I realize now that this has created lots of extra work for you. I plan to be more attentive to restoring the space before locking up."

- "I lost my temper at the staff meeting and yelled at you, and I wish I hadn't. It was unprofessional on my part. I am sorry; I'm going to work hard to make sure it doesn't happen again."

- "You've been trying to reach me for a month and I've not returned your calls; I'm sorry about that. My goal for myself is to return calls within forty-eight hours, and I am renewing my commitment to that goal right now."

Beyond "I'm Sorry": Making Amends

I am not one to say "words are cheap." As anyone who has uttered "I'm sorry" knows, sincere apologies are costly. They come from the depths of a bruised identity and can leave one feeling vulnerable and exposed. But when you recognize that your choices have hurt another, saying "I'm sorry" alone will often not be enough to repair the relationship. It is the beginning of repentance but not the end. The other person still has a range of feelings he wants to express, and part of repentance is being able to hear out the other person without offering defenses or excuses for our behavior.

We have already talked about ways of receiving the strong emotions of others in chapter 5. Tutu refers to this stage in the process as being willing to "witness another's anguish." Acknowledging that often anguish is couched in language of accusation and blame, he nevertheless says, "The best way to do this is to not argue the facts of their stories or the ways they are hurting. If your spouse says you lied last Wednesday, and you lied to them last Thursday, it will not help rebuild the trust by arguing the date of the offense. . . . When people are hurting, they cannot be cross-examined out of their pain."[6] Sometimes we may need to say "I'm sorry" several times before the apology begins to be heard and believed by the other.

Tutu recommends specifically asking for forgiveness as a sign of acknowledging one's responsibility and wish to repair the relationship. As discussed earlier, forgiveness is always a gift, and the other person might not have it to give yet. Just as it would erase the power of an apology if we said we were sorry when not sincere, it erases the power of forgiveness if it is pronounced when not really present. The "good news" (if one is allowed to call it that) is that repentance isn't contingent upon being forgiven. Tutu says, "The fact that you will not be forgiven in the way you wish does not have to prevent your own growth and healing. None of us can continue to bear the burden of a wrong for which we are truly penitent and contrite."[7]

What repentance *does* demand is the willingness to make amends. Words can express remorse, but actions demonstrate the sincerity of our remorse.[8] Appropriate amends will vary depending on the nature of the offense. If money was lost, money can be repaid. Property damaged can be fixed. The spouse of an alcoholic may need to hear, "I will never drink again," and then see it. The teen who has created grief for her family may commit to counseling and do it. Last year, I heard the powerful story of a religious community who accompanied one of its members to a police station in another country so he could turn himself in for an allegation of sexual abuse from two decades ago. Making amends cannot assure forgiveness, but alongside apology, it is the most likely route to healing on both sides.

But What If It's Not "My Fault"?

Fair enough. It's not like you've been sitting around all day twiddling your thumbs. If you've not returned my calls or cleaned up the gathering space, it is because you are doing what used to be three peoples' jobs and then going to the hospital to visit your friend's grandfather. How were you supposed to know the fish was bad? Wouldn't anyone lose her temper under this kind of stress? It's important that in our minds we not confuse the gift of accountability with blame, though admittedly, the two often come to us from others wrapped in the same package.

Christian moral theology commonly analyzes the actions people do in terms of three factors: the action itself (what we did), the intention behind the action (why we did it), and the circumstances surrounding the action (where, with whom, under what conditions, consequences, etc.). The degree of moral culpability—or the amount of personal "blame" one holds for an act—depends on all three of these factors in conjunction with one another. There are times when looking back I might realize that the action I chose was the wrong one, I had a bad intention when choosing it, and there was nothing stopping me from making another, better decision. In these situations the tradition would say I am fully culpable—the blame is all mine.

It is generally much more complicated than that though, isn't it? With hindsight, we recognize the choice was the wrong one to make and we wish we'd done something different, but our intention was good or there were circumstances surrounding the decision that made it difficult to choose anything else. I knew that leaving the hall a mess was not kind to the next person who walked in there, but my intention was not to cause harm; I needed to go pick up my kids from the sitter, and it would also be problematic to leave her waiting when she has her own kids to put to bed. I agree serving poisoned food to a guest is just plain wrong, but I had no idea the fish had spoiled.

Accepting the gift of accountability is not necessarily synonymous with accepting "blame" in a situation.

In much of daily life, we are blamed for things that, from our perspective, we had little control over. But we can still feel remorse for outcomes we did not intend, and we can still apologize for the impact our actions had on others, even if we are not necessarily morally "culpable." Simply put, it is good and sometimes necessary to repent for "mistakes" as well as "sins."

This is not the same as saying we need to take ownership for every messy, hurtful situation we find ourselves in. In accepting the gift of accountability, we own up to *our* contribution to the overall problem—in essence, to the role *we* played, to the choices *we* made—while recognizing there were other factors involved. Often the other person has also made contributions to the problem, for which he or she can take ownership. And often, there are factors beyond both of our control (freakish weather, unanticipated traffic, policies made by "higher ups," the limitations of time and space, etc.). Rather than framing the conversation in terms of who is to blame, we can shift it to be as honest as possible about all of the factors that contributed to it, including our own but not limited to our own.

- "So I agree, this situation is a real mess and I know I contributed to it. Specifically, I did ___ and ___, and I am really sorry for that. Are there other contributions you think I've made that I've not mentioned? Can we also talk about some of the other things that I think were at play here?"

- "I realize now that there was a lot more at stake for you in this decision than I was aware of. I wish I'd asked more questions in advance and I take ownership of that. I don't think the decision itself was necessarily the wrong one to make, but I do think my lack of asking for input before making it was wrong, and in the future, I am going to ask more questions."

- "Can I just say upfront that I am sorry for the role I played in this? I _____. I didn't mean for it to lead to this, but I can see how it has."

The Face of Reconciliation

This chapter and the last have described two separate but complementary practices that lie at the core of the Christian Gospel. They can take place separately from one another: it is possible to forgive even if the other never repents, and it is possible to repent even if never forgiven. But when repentance and forgiveness do meet, an amazing thing happens: reconciliation.

Reconciliation does not necessarily mean that the relationship between the parties will be reestablished. Sometimes, on this side of Parousia, that might not be able to happen. The best we can hope for is that both have reached a state of peace in which memories of the past no longer continue to harm in the present. But in many situations, reconciliation does mean the renewal and deepening of relationship. It will not be the same relationship as the one before but rather a "new creation"—a sign of God's constant, ongoing work to heal and transform the earth.

God never wills for bad things to happen to us and to our relationships. But the power of God is such that when bad things do happen—when our choices fracture rather than unite—the relationships that emerge through reconciliation can be even stronger than the ones that existed before. Our friendships, our marriages, our communities find themselves even more tightly woven and resilient not because we are so deserving but because God is *that good*.

Companions for the Journey:
Joseph Green and Ann Putnam

The tiny town of Danvers, Massachusetts, lies about an hour's drive north of Boston in the shadow of its more well-known sister suburb Salem, about seven miles away. Salem makes a business of its notorious history—even the police cars are marked with the silhouette of witches riding brooms. But quiet Danvers, the site where most of the accusers and accused actually lived, remembers the 1692 witch trials in a more solemn, understated way. On the wall of the homestead of Rebecca Nurse—a seventy-one-year-old hung in the gallows—is a sign for the curious tourist: "How many witches were put to death here?" it asks. Below it replies, "None, but many innocent people were jailed, falsely convicted, and nineteen were executed."

Much has been written on the hysteria that swept the early Puritan colony and the multiple factors that played a role in the outbreak of allegations. What is much less known is the story of how the community healed in the wake of the trials. Here were neighbors whose daughters had accused others' wives, whose wives had accused local widows. Indeed in one case, there was a husband who had accused his own spouse. And on Sunday, they were all supposed to pray with one another?

On the Danvers corner where the original Salem community worshiped, there now stands another humble marker reading, "To this church rent by the witchcraft frenzy, came in 1697, the Reverend Joseph Green, aged twenty-two. He induced the mischief makers to confess, reconciled the factions, established the first public school, and became noted for his skill at hunting game and his generous hospitality."

How did Joseph Green manage all this? A recent seminary graduate from Cambridge, Green was not by nature a bookworm but an outdoorsman who readily socialized with townsfolk and got to know them as friends. From his earliest days with the community, he recognized the need for healing. The executed had also been excommunicated, and their families (not surprisingly) were no longer active in the church. Only weeks after his ordination, he wrote in the church record:

> November 25, 1698 . . . I desired the church to man-
> ifest by the usual sign that they were so cordially
> satisfied with their brethren Thomas Wilkins, John
> Tarbell, and Samuel Nurse that they were heartily
> desirous that they would join with us in all ordi-
> nances, that so we might live lovingly together.
> . . . And further that whatever articles they had
> drawn up against these brethren formerly, they
> now looked upon them as nothing, but let them
> fall to the ground, being willing that they should
> be buried forever.[9]

Green visited the families of the victims and invited them personally back to services. Already by February 1699, he happily reports that Wilkins, Tarbell, and Nurse had "joined with us in the Lord's supper, which is a matter of thankfulness, seeing they have for a long time been so offended as that they could not comfortably live with us."[10]

He arranged seating in the church so that the families of the accused and the accusers were placed side by side and began to interact more with each other.

Reconciliation was a slow process, however. In February 1704, Green grew more daring and suggested that the church strike from its record the excommunication of one of its former members, Martha Corey, executed for witchcraft. While many agreed, a few vocal members did not—thinking that if the accused was not guilty of witchcraft, it would mean the accusers were guilty of murder. They were not ready for that degree of ownership of the events. The town meeting in which this conversation was held became so heated and ended in such bitterness that Green swore he'd never go to another, but he did not back away from the larger vision of healing. Having reached out to those who'd been injured by the witchcraft accusations, he knew he still had more work to do with those who had been among the accusers.

A turning point came in 1706 when Ann Putnam, one of the original accusers, decided she wanted to ask forgiveness for what she had done. Ann had been twelve years old when the hysteria began, the child of a tense and unhappy home life. She and her troubled mother dominated the trials with their theatrics. She alone accused sixty-two people. When both her parents died within weeks of each other in 1699, nineteen-year-old Ann was left to raise her nine younger siblings. Deeply burdened by both her duties and a growing sense of guilt, Ann's health took a turn for the worse. She reached out to Green and to Samuel Nurse, Rebecca's son, who represented the families of the victims.

With Green's help, Putnam wrote out and signed her confession, which Green then read before the assembly on August 25. Using language common for the time, Putnam claimed that she'd been "deluded by Satan" and was an "ignorant and unwitting . . . instrument"—not language that we know to be helpful in an apology today. But Putnam did acknowledge that her actions had led to the death of innocent persons. "And particularly," she noted, "as I was a chief instrument of accusing Goodwife Nurse and her two sisters, I desire to lie in the dust and be humbled for it, in that I was a cause, with others, of so sad a calamity to them and their families. . . . I earnestly beg forgiveness of God and from all those unto whom I have given just cause of sorrow and offense."[11]

She was the only one of the accusers to make such an apology, but the sentiment went a long way. The community eventually agreed to have Rebecca Nurse's excommunication blotted from the church record. It was no longer a source of debate.

Green and Putnam, who were born within years of each other, also died within years of each other—Green in 1715 at the age of forty and Putnam in 1716 at the age of thirty-seven. But their church community, healed of its bitterness, went on.

For **Reflection** *and* **Prayer**

1. Can you think of a time in your own life where accountability arrived as a "gift"? Did it feel like a gift at the time or is it something that only dawned on you later? What helped you to recognize it as "gift"?

2. What patterns do you note in your own life regarding taking ownership of your contribution and apologizing? Is it something that comes easy to

you? Hard? Frequent? Infrequent? If you could change something about your pattern, what would it be?

3. In your experience, has it been worth it still to repent, even if not forgiven by the other? What have been the benefits of repentance in your life?

4. What insights does the story of reconciliation in Danvers offer as you reflect on your own efforts to "repent"?

It is easy for me to tell you, my God, that I am
      sorry.
With you, the words slip out easily and fearlessly,
for you already know all and promise mercy.
But, now, my God, I need you to stir within me
the courage to speak such words to another
where no such promises exist,
another who cannot see me with your eyes.
Embolden me to make right what I have done
      wrong;
to listen to what is painful to hear;
and to begin walking a new path in life,
even if the other is not able to forgive me.
Amen.

10. Problem Solve

In everything do to others as you would
have them do to you;
for this is the law and the prophets.

—Matthew 7:12

Several years ago, we had a significant conversation in
the community where I worship about how we pray
with one another. I realize that outside the church, it
must sound mighty odd to hear that Christians argue
about who sits where, who gets to do what, and
whether we will use this language or that when we
gather on Sundays. But anyone who's been in a church
for longer than a month will quickly recognize these are
some of the most painful and protracted disagreements
we have. In fact, we finally brought in someone from
the outside to help facilitate the conversation for us
because it was so tough.

And we had a really good conversation. At the
end of the session, we understood each other's points
of view much better. We grasped what was motivating the various factions and what they understood to
be at stake. We did a great job separating intent from

impact—acknowledging that just because some felt excluded, it wasn't because others intended their words and actions to make them feel that way. Many who were part of the conversation afterward referred to it as The Great Thaw because relationships that had been icy seemed to melt a bit, giving new hope.

And then nothing changed.

Those who had been hurt thought that once they'd expressed the impact of others' choices on them, the offenders would do things differently. And those who'd done the offending thought that once they'd explained they meant no harm, others would stop being hurt. A cold wind began to blow through the community again, threatening to refreeze what had defrosted. Understanding had taken us so far, but we had neglected to build into the original conversation a time for talking about *next steps*. We weren't finished with this conversation. It would be necessary to gather again.

In chapter 2, we identified three good reasons to engage in a tough conversation: to learn more, to speak one's own insight, and to invite the other into a different sort of future by problem solving together. In this chapter, we'll look more closely at the last of these purposes. And, just as we've discovered with so many of the other topics in this book, when broaching the topic of problem solving there are certain polarizing tendencies we want to avoid.

Stay Away from the Gutters

In the game of bowling, there is a broad alley down which the ball can comfortably roll, but on either side of the alley there are gutters that let you know you are leaning too far in one direction or the other.

The first set of "gutters" in the world of problem solving would be the "Fix It Now" vs. "It's Unfixable" ruts.

In one gutter are those of us who are tempted to jump to problem solving immediately. (Indeed, maybe for some readers this is the chapter of the book you flip to first!) As soon as someone raises something troubling, we want to leap in and figure out how to fix it. Although filled with goodwill, we race to answers without slowing down enough to listen and understand. As a result, responses are sometimes haphazard and off-target, doing little to address the presenting problem.

In the other gutter are those of us who dismiss problem solving as something not worth pursuing. Perhaps out of previous experience or messages passed on since early childhood, we assume the problem is unsolvable, saying things like, "We tried addressing this before and nothing happened." "It probably won't work." "There's nothing I can do to change this." We have extended meetings where we revisit familiar frustrations but leave with no action items.

A quick scan through the early chapters of Genesis
suffices to suggest that the God of the Judeo-Christian
tradition operates throughout history in the wide-open
"alley" between those extremes. When the first humans
eat of the forbidden tree, God does not race in to fix the
situation but neither does God give up Adam and Eve
as a lost cause, instead sewing them some clothes and
helping them as they figure out how to live with the
consequences. God watches as sin spreads and ravages
the earth and decides to wash it away with a flood.
But God doesn't abandon the project of creation alto-
gether, instead renewing it through Noah and his ark.
Sin rears its ugly head again, and God says, "Let me
try to reform from within the human race by calling
forth Abraham and making of him a new people." The
story told by the rest of scripture proceeds in a similar
fashion. Over and over, we meet a God who tinkers
and tweaks but never gives up, remaining creative long
after the seventh day of creation. We meet a God who
redeems. And this God is constantly inviting humans
to be ongoing partners in problem solving, allies in
renewing the plotline of planet earth.

A second set of "ruts," however, presents a nar-
rower path to traverse, if not quite a needle's eye. It
has to do with one's problem-solving approach. On
one side of this split, we find those who "drive a hard
bargain." They are clear about what they want to see
happen and are willing to do whatever is necessary to
push that agenda through, including behind-your-back

deals, pressuring for concessions, making threats, and public shaming. We could say they are "hard on the problem" and are often successful in getting what they want. But they are also "hard on the people"—the relationship they have with their problem-solving partners suffers.

There is something about this approach that is inherently at odds with Christianity. Most of us recognize that the "end" of this style of problem solving might be a great good—for example, a piece of valuable legislation pushed through that will truly better society—but it has been won by means that are not consonant with the outcome. If we recognize God's final plan for us is communion, we ultimately undercut that plan whenever we hurt relationships. It might appear we've won a "battle," but we are losing "the war." We may think that we will never need to problem solve with a particular partner again in the future and so how they feel treated by us doesn't matter, but the world is an increasingly small place. Chances are we *will* encounter this partner or someone they know again, and our reputation will precede us. Jesus's admonition to treat others as we would like to be treated is not only spiritually edifying but also pragmatically sound.

On the other side of this split, then, we will find the "soft bargainers." They value the relationship with the other so highly that they will quickly make concessions to accommodate the other's will. They are transparent, trusting, open, and easy to deal with. Rather than a victory, they are looking for an agreement and willing to do whatever necessary to make everyone happy, even at the cost of their own interests. They are "soft on people." But they are also "soft on the problem." In the effort to be kind, they make little progress on the issues at hand.

While some might think this approach is more consonant with Christianity, it is equally problematic. Nowhere in scripture is "niceness" lifted up as a necessary virtue. Rather, Christians are called to be faithful to their values, to be leaven in society and light in the world. We are supposed to be agents of change, not pushovers.

The narrow path we seek to walk as Christians is one in which we can be "soft on people" but "hard on problems." Roger Fisher and William Ury, founding members of the Harvard Negotiation Project who first framed the challenge in these terms, speak of this narrow path as the path of "principled negotiation."[1] They note, "People often assume that there is a trade-off between pursuing a good substantive outcome and pursuing a good relationship. We disagree. A good working relationship tends to make it easier to get good substantive outcomes (for both sides). Good substantive outcomes tend to make a good relationship even better."[2]

So how can we problem solve in a way that makes progress on the issue at hand *and* honors the dignity of those involved at the same time?

Separate the Person from the Problem

In times of conflict, Fisher and Ury highlight, we naturally conflate the problem we are having and the person with whom we are having the problem.[3] They become one in our mind. In fact, the problem exists *in the space between* the two parties.

Let's say I run a housing program for women who have recently been released from prison. The program has a strict policy about the women not using drugs or alcohol while they are living in program housing. One night, Lucy comes home drunk. Indeed, for argument's sake, let's say she is carrying a half-empty bottle of tequila in her hand as she walks in the kitchen door. Now, clearly, this is a problem. Indeed, watching her stumble through the doorway, the problem feels like a baseball coming in my direction at ninety miles an hour. And my first thought is that the problem is Lucy. But the problem is not Lucy. The problem is the drunkenness and the fact that this drunkenness violates the policy of the housing program. If I were not managing this program or if Lucy were not living here, this would not be a problem for me. It would be a problem for someone else, but not for me. This problem lies at the intersection of her behavior and how I understand my responsibilities.

Separating the people from the problem means that I "catch" the problem, not unlike I would catch a baseball if I were crouched behind home plate. But then

instead of tossing it back, I walk over to the pitcher—
in this case, Lucy—and say, "Hey, let's look at this
together." I hold the problem separate from the two of
us. In my mind, rather than visualize her in front of me,
I visualize her beside me, also looking at this problem
as my ally in trying to figure out what to do about it.

- "Lucy, this housing community has a policy that
  residents cannot drink alcohol while living here,
  and last night you came home drunk. I want you at
  my side to help figure out next steps about where
  we go from here."

In this situation, I may hold much of the decision-making power as to whether or not Lucy remains
in this particular housing program, but the problem to
solve is larger than merely the question of her housing
right now, and I want to communicate that I am still
on her side, even if part of what I need to let her know
in this conversation is that living here is no longer one
of the options.

The example given is a rather dramatic one, but
the principle still holds even in the most mundane of
circumstances.

- "We've had a couple of community meetings now
  that have somehow touched upon the pileup of
  dirty coffee mugs in the common kitchen, but
  we've not tackled this problem directly. Can we talk
  about what's going on with our use of the kitchen

and come up with some possible solutions to test together?"

Distinguish between Positions and Interests

Remember the "ladder of inference" from chapter 3? Argyris's construct can be helpful when in problem-solving mode as well. When we begin to pose possible solutions to the difficulties we are facing, we often start at the top of the ladder with our conclusions about what we think should or should not be done. In the realm of problem-solving, Fisher and Ury refer to these conclusions as "positions."[4]

- "There is no way that we can have the annual Boy Scout pancake breakfast on the last Saturday of the month because that is when we promised to have the food pantry open."

- "We absolutely must repave the parking lot this year."

In problem solving, we frequently take these positions at face value and begin to immediately argue with them or barter with them.

- "Fine; then we get the hall on Sunday and Girl Scout cookie distribution has to move to the garage."

- "No, the beautification budget this year has to be used to redo the meditation garden. The garden's been on the waiting list for funding now for three years."

Underneath such positions, however, lie interests. "Your position is something you have decided upon," say Fisher and Ury. "Your interests are what caused you to so decide."[5] Ironically, many of our interests are aligned, even when we hold differing positions about the best way to proceed. We are both interested in the beautification of the property—we want this to be a place to which people are attracted to come. We all care about the kids in our community *and* we care about the hungry. We even all care about having a clean kitchen sink, free of dirty coffee mugs, more or less. Both Lucy and I want her to have a positive future that involves a safe place to live and somehow does not boomerang back toward prison. Naming interests aloud can help reinforce the earlier notion of separating the people from the problem; we realize how much we share in common with each other and not just our differences.

But just as valuable, naming our interests illumines what is most important to us, and sometimes what is most important to us might be had in ways other than the positions we've staked out. As the one who runs the food pantry, it is important to me that we are open on the last Saturday because that is the time of the month when peoples' food stamps run out. But where we distribute the food from doesn't matter so much. As the pack leader of the Boy Scouts, I'm not wedded to the last Saturday, but my interest is not to overlap other events that troop members are likely to be engaged in, and I really need the hall. It is the only space large enough to host the number of people we are expecting. In order to be "hard" on problems, we should hold on to our interests, though not necessarily our positions.

The best way to build relationship in the middle of problem solving is to show concern for the others' interests, even if we aren't inclined to agree to their positions. And the only way to get at interests is to ask about them.

- "You seem really insistent about the food pantry using the hall on the last Saturday of the month. Is it specifically the last Saturday that matters or could it be another Saturday? Does the location matter to you or could it be elsewhere?"

- "I want to make sure I understand your interests here. Why is repaving the parking lot at the top of your priority list?"

From a principled negotiation standpoint, the optimal agreement would be one that meets as many of both of your interests as it possibly can, not merely your own and not merely theirs. Don't make an agreement unless the agreement makes sense for both parties and not just for one. The irony is that in discovering the other's interests, you will often find he has some interests that you can happily meet because they require no or little cost to you. You are able to build the goodwill in the relationship without sacrificing the substance of your own interests. And that happens by moving from the question of interests to the question of options.

Generate Options Before Moving to Action

Earlier in this chapter, we talked about the compulsion many of us suffer to leap immediately into "fix-it" mode. I have long loved the story of Solomon in scripture who, when confronted with two mothers battling over a single infant, said, "Get me a sword! Cut the living child in two, and give half to one woman and half to the other" (1 Kgs 3:24–25). Now Solomon is of course noted for his wisdom. Note how quickly his words served to separate positions from interests. Immediately, it becomes clear which woman is the true "mother" to the child, whether the biological mother or not, for one agrees to the preposterous proposal whereas the other's interest *is* the child. But Solomon's words also illumine the flaw behind the typical way we seek to solve problems when in a hurry: just split it in half. "Can't you just share?" we shout to our children in the backseat. "Should we just split the check?" we ask. Lots of times this proposal makes sense, and it certainly is the fastest way of handling things. But equal does not always mean fair. And, in the case of Solomon and the two mothers, equal would also mean death. Truly no one would have their interests met.

Fisher and Ury talk about slowing down the leap from spotting the problem to acting on it by pausing to consider additional options.[6] It seems like such a simple, common-sense suggestion, but when under pressure, we forget to do it. The only ideas that rush to mind are "I win," "you win," or "we cut it in half." If we know each other's interests, it's possible that there are *lots* of ways we could both win, but that requires the freedom to brainstorm. Fisher and Ury's key insight is that brainstorming must be separated from deciding.[7] In brainstorming mode, we are just tossing out possible ideas but not criticizing them or actually holding ourselves to them. If possible, all ideas should be written out in full view, so that they can be looked at again.

- "So one option is that we use the whole of the beautification budget this year on the parking lot. Another option is that we use all of it on the meditation garden. We could split the monies in half. I bet we can think of some other options, too . . . We could go together to the finance committee and ask them to double our budget. What else could we try?"

- "I don't know, I'm just dreaming here and am not wedded to any of this, but maybe the Boy Scouts could help move bags of food for this month's food pantry over to another location on the campus so that the scouts could use the hall but the pantry still stay open. Maybe we could ask families coming to the pancake breakfast to bring a canned good with them. Maybe we could . . ."

Only at the close of brainstorming, ask which ideas seem most promising—again, not to make any commitments yet but just to identify which ones you might want to think about further. Invite ideas that would strengthen promising ideas.

- "Lucy, I like the idea of you looking at a residential addiction program rather than moving back in with your aunt. Can we talk about that option some more? What would make that route even more attractive? More doable?"

- "I love the idea of installing a dishwasher—that makes a lot of sense to me, but I know it also has to make sense in the wider budget. Is there anything that would make that option more feasible?"

Sometimes options will need more research and consideration. You might not reach an agreement about the best way forward in a single conversation. But do set a time by which a decision will be made and communicated about what will be tried next, even if the decision is "we aren't going to change anything right now." There are few things more frustrating than getting as far as brainstorming and then having the conversation simply drop, never arriving at a commitment to any action. Decisions don't need to be perfect or permanent to be actionable. They can be viewed as experiments.

- "Let's try rotating dishwashing duty for a month and see how it goes. If we don't like it, we can revisit this conversation again in October."

- "So you'll call your aunt and I'll ask my social work buddy about residential addiction treatment places that might have an opening. Let's compare notes tomorrow morning and decide on the next step."

Even if what you decide to try doesn't end up being the final solution that resolves the problem once and for all, it is okay. Remember God has that problem, too. We keep tweaking. We keep tempering. We keep attacking the problem while respecting the persons involved. We keep participating in the ongoing work of redeeming.

Companions for the Journey:
The Congregation of Dom Saint Petri

Dom Saint Petri has sat atop the highest point above the River Spree in the tiny town of Bautzen since somewhere around the year AD 1000. Legend has it was founded by Bishop Benno, the first missionary to the Sorbs, a Slavic community that settled in this region of what is now far eastern Germany, near the Czech and Polish borders. The axis of the cathedral is oddly bent, and no one knows quite why. Perhaps it was constructed such merely to fit a bend in the town's road. But, the crook in the architecture serves also as a metaphor for the history of the church's congregation, which has been anything but ordinary.

Eastern Germany was one of the first areas impacted by the Protestant Reformation in the early 1500s. Indeed, Martin Luther nailed his famed ninety-five theses to the door of the church in Wittenberg just over a hundred miles away. The ideas of the reform spread rapidly through the region as the worship practices of towns frequently shifted back and forth according to the leanings of the local prince. Throughout Europe, the debate of ideas soon came to be accompanied by violence and destruction. Many church buildings were purged of their sacred artifacts and images, and some were burnt to the ground. As far away as England, one bishop records,

> What clattering of glasses! What beating down of walls! What wresting out of irons and brass from the windows! What demolishing of curious stonework! What tooting and piping upon organ pipes! And what a hideous triumph, when all the mangled organ pipes, vestments, together with the leaden cross which had newly been sawn down from the pulpit and the service books that could be carried to the fire in the public marketplace were heaped together.[8]

But as Europe experienced over a hundred years of turmoil, the crooked church of Bautzen, in the eye of the storm, remained strangely unscathed. Why?

In 1523, as tension was building between Roman Catholic and protesting communities, options appeared limited. The energy of the times seemed to favor the protestors. The official stance of the Catholic hierarchy was to refuse any accommodation of Protestant demands. But the Catholic bishop of Dom Saint Petri was not one to be constrained by a win-lose mentality: he invited the protestors to share the cathedral. The move was an unorthodox one that could have brought him trouble with his own superiors. And the protestors did not need to accept; indeed, they had the upper hand in the region. But surprisingly, both sides agreed to give it a try. Within the church building, they built a wall to separate the Catholic and Lutheran worship spaces and created one of the first *simultankirche*—or "simultaneous" churches—in the world and the only one in eastern Germany. In 1543, with religious competition increasing all around Bautzen, they signed a formal contract that still governs the joint use of space and times of the services even to this day.

For the past five hundred years, the Lutheran and Catholic congregation of Dom Saint Petri has practiced the "ecumenism of daily life." The cathedral still has two separate altars, two separate organs, and two separate times of worship, but both parties share joint responsibility for the upkeep and maintenance of the building, and that has not always been easy. In 1643, the church suffered a severe fire, but the Lutherans and Catholics rebuilt it together. Since then, they've had to agree about the installation of a single furnace system and electricity, the replacement of organs and windows, the care of the bells and the artwork, and when it was time to repaint. And slowly, this ongoing collaboration has lowered the wall between them—literally. What used to be a thirteen-foot-high solid barrier in the middle of the church is now a three-foot-high decorative fence, with an unlocked gate through which congregants and visitors pass back and forth with ease. Perhaps soon, the congregation hopes, it will come down all together.

For **Reflection** *and* **Prayer**

1. Can you think of a time in your own life when you thought you'd reached a new level of understanding with someone, and then nothing changed? Did you give up on the conversation or re-engage it? To what effect?

2. Do you tend to get more feedback that you are "hard on problems and also hard on people" or "soft on problems and also soft on people"? What do you find most promising about the practice

of being "hard on problems but soft on people"? What do you find most intimidating?

3. When you think about the most challenging situation you are facing right now, what kinds of options might you begin to consider beyond "your way, my way, or cut it in half"?

4. When you read the story of Dom Saint Petri, what is one insight you would like to carry forward into a tough situation you are facing in your own life?

Ever-creative God, your imagination has no
     limits.
Where I see black or white, you paint a rainbow of
     options.
Where I propose a or b, you take delight in crying,
     "All of the above!"
I should like a good dose of your creativity right
     now, O Lord,
as I try to look anew at the circumstances I find
     most challenging.
I want you to expand my imagination
to see possibilities that at present I just can't see—
possibilities not tried before.
I want you to also open my ears,
so that should another see a way forward that I do
     not,
I can be receptive to that voice,
even if it is spoken by the one I least want to hear
     right now.
Amen.

11. Be Trustworthy,
Not Necessarily Trusting

See, I am sending you out like sheep into
the midst of wolves;
so be wise as serpents and innocent as
doves.

—Matthew 10:16

In scripture, over and over again we see that God's word and God's action are synonymous. When God says, "Let there be light," there is light. But with humans it is not always so. We say one thing and do another. We make promises and don't keep them. And Jesus knew that. Jesus knew that the world can be a hard and cruel place. He knew that people aren't always fair. That those with power often abuse it. That some people can look you right in the eye and lie, and think they are doing what is best. Jesus was no fool. He knew.

Jesus told his disciples that, in the face of all that was duplicitous, they still needed to model truth and justice in all things. Like God, their words and their actions needed to be entirely aligned. They needed to say "yes" when they meant yes and "no" when they meant no (see Mt 5:37). They needed to treat others as they would want to be treated (see Mt 7:12). But at no point in time did he promise them that if they practiced what he taught, the favor of truth and justice would be returned by others. His disciples should be trustworthy but not necessarily trusting.

In chapter 10, we talked about being principled in our own approach to problem solving. In this chapter, we consider what to do when we sense the other may not be returning the favor. Maybe we suspect outright duplicitousness. Or maybe we sense the other's heart *is* in the right place but eagerness to be hard on the issue makes him unaware of the impact he is having. The most natural human response in these situations is to turn the golden rule on its head and begin to treat the other as he has treated us, perhaps thinking this will help "teach him a lesson." But as negotiation scholars Roger Fisher and William Ury note,

> There is no need to emulate unconstructive behavior. Doing so may indeed "teach them a lesson," though often not the lesson we would like. In most cases responding in kind reinforces the behavior we dislike. It encourages the other side to feel that everyone behaves that way, and that it is the only way to protect themselves. Our behavior should be designed to model and encourage the behavior we

would prefer and to avoid any reward for behavior we dislike.[1]

Basically, there are ways to break a pattern of interaction that feels unfair or deceitful other than imitating or participating in it.

Seek Fair Criteria

Fisher and Ury observe that many times in problem solving the parties try to resolve their differences merely on the basis of "will"—in other words, by discussing what they are willing or unwilling to put up with.[2]

- "The chaplains in your department only saw 60 percent of the patients who came to the hospital this year. That's unacceptable. I expect that at least 90 percent will be seen! This needs to be number one on your performance goals for the coming year."

- "We were really impressed with your resume and interview and want to offer you the job, but our budget is only $____. We're hoping you'll still say 'yes.'"

There are many virtues that we are called upon to exercise in the Christian life, including generosity, magnanimity, diligence in work, and so forth, but in negotiating mode, the most foundational concern needs to be justice, or as Thomas Aquinas defined it, "giving each person his due."[3] The pursuit of justice is important in problem solving not because it is rated as the number one virtue on any sort of divine checklist but because, from a purely pragmatic standpoint, an agreement is unlikely to stand the test of time unless both parties believe it to be fair. Sometimes in a bind, we might arrive at a temporary Band-Aid solution, but over time, ongoing relationships that aren't perceived by both parties as just tend to breed resentment, frustration, and even the duplicity mentioned earlier.

Rather than frame the effort at reaching agreement in terms of what each person is willing to do, justice is aided by identifying "objective criteria"[4] that can be established independent of the parties and what each wants.

- "Knowing how much we each value the patients' spiritual care, I imagine we'd both love to see the number at 100 percent! But, in terms of deciding my performance goals for next year, why don't we look to see if there are norms the chaplains' association has documented from hospitals across the country? We could see what the average is for hospitals with a similar chaplain/patient ratio to our own."

- "In my ideal world, I'd be earning $____, and I am guessing it'd be ideal for the ministry's budget to pay minimum wage. So rather than talking about what's ideal, perhaps the most helpful thing would be to try to figure out what seems just. I know there are some professional organizations that give normal wage ranges for this kind of position in various parts of the country. Before putting any numbers out on the table, why don't we look at these as a starting place for a salary conversation?"

There is a plethora of objective standards that can serve as resources when negotiating, e.g., the Kelley Blue Book, a licensed property appraisal company, or diocesan or professional association salary scales. It depends on the issue, but in many cases, there exists more than a single standard that might be used to evaluate the worthiness of a proposal. Part of the conversation may need to be deciding what tool best applies in the situation at hand. But simply by having the conversation, you will have shifted the negotiation to more promising ground.

Talk about Doubts

You'd like to believe what the other person is telling you—that he will follow through on his promise, that her solution will work just as planned, that he's heard you and things will be different now. But sometimes you don't. There is a nagging voice inside your head saying, "Yeah, I've heard that before." "That will never work." "When hell freezes over." To doubt is not necessarily a bad thing. Indeed, it is a healthy impulse that keeps us from making bad decisions and getting trapped in harmful relationships. Sometimes, as

Christians, we hear Jesus's words to Thomas about the blessedness of those who are able to believe without seeing[5] and think it is advice for how to live all of life. One quick survey of Church history—never mind human history—and all the evil that has taken place when people have not voiced their doubts, and we can rest assured that the meaning of the Thomas story must be interpreted in a very specific and limited way.

The broader Christian tradition acknowledges that doubt arrives as a divine gift to let us know something is not quite aligned with God's dream for us. To refer back to an image from chapter 2, the questions that trouble our minds are not to be dismissed but rather viewed as the crooked finger of God. In an interview, Mother Teresa of Kolkata once noted that if a person has no questions in her mind, it may well be that God is reaching her exactly where she is. But the moment that a person has a question, that question is a grace. It is God beckoning, "Come along now. . . . Keep thinking. Keep wondering. You are not quite where I want you to be yet." And so, each person is obligated to pursue his or her questions until reaching a state of peace. Mother Teresa gave this answer in response to a query about the people she served from varying religions.[6] But I think her response also makes sense much more broadly. When we have questions in any sort of relationship, when something doesn't quite make sense, we are being unfaithful to the relationship to ignore those questions and pretend they aren't there.

Raising doubts when problem solving and naming what would help you to resolve your doubts increases the chance of arriving at a sustainable solution with which you will feel comfortable.

- "I want to believe you when you say____, and at the same time here's the data I've got running through my mind that raises my suspicions: _____. Can you talk specifically to those points?"

- "You've raised some good points, and I'm still not persuaded. Let me tell you what would persuade me to think differently about this: ____."

Furthermore, if you are having a hard time making progress in problem solving with another party, know that it may be because that person, too, has doubts. It's possible she has also seen things that make it hard for her to trust. Inviting her to name her doubts in the open and asking what she would find persuasive can sometimes break through the impasse.

- "I've given you all the reasons I can think of as to why I think ___ is the best option, but I'm sensing that you're not persuaded. Can you tell me what would persuade you? What would you want to see before being willing to give ____ a try?"

- "You've mentioned some things about the proposal that make you nervous. I want to make sure you feel safe in signing onto this. What could we build into the agreement to make it feel more trustworthy to you?"

Name the Game

Often in the middle of problem solving, you might be struck by the intuition, "Hey, we're not playing fair here." It is not only a question as to whether what's been proposed seems unfair but about whether the conversation itself seems unfair. Perhaps each time you've made a requested concession and think that you've arrived at an agreement, the other wants just one more concession. Perhaps you are having a tough time finding common ground, and the other starts issuing threats. Perhaps you are focused on the future, and the other starts bringing up issues from the past again.

One of the hardest things to do when we are uncomfortable with the tenor of a conversation is "name the game." In the moment, we are often unaware of the strategies the other is engaging in his problem-solving approach. We are listening to what he is saying and we have a gut sense of being manipulated, but we unconsciously get sucked into playing the game before we realize we are playing it. He barks and, before thinking, we bite.

- "If you won't let me choose the songs for the Christmas program, then I'll quit directing the choir."

> "That's fine, but if you quit directing the choir, your kids will lose their tuition discount at the school."

- "So I just got confirmation from the pastor that we can bend the rules a bit and rent you the hall for your wedding reception for \$___, with no extra charge for the hour before to set up or for the use of the sound system."

> "What about some extra time at the end, though, for cleanup?"

> "I didn't ask about that. Let me go back and check."

While it is hard to do, "naming the game" can be a far more effective response. If we can pause to become aware our gut is trying to tell us something, we can step back and identify for ourselves and for the other person the problem-solving approach we find troubling.

- "A couple of times now when I've raised choir-related issues you've threatened to quit over it. Maybe there is something you find really unsatisfying about the work, in which case I want to hear about it. But in terms of problem solving, the strategy of saying 'I'm going to quit' whenever I raise a concern feels manipulative to me. I'd like to figure out another way of talking about our disagreements."

- "My perception is that each time I think we've settled on an agreement, you have additional things
  you'd like to include. This pattern of back-and-forth
  is creating challenges for me, and I'd like to figure
  out another way of arriving at a contract both sides
  can agree is fair and can say 'yes' to."

In the inimitable phrasing of Fisher and Ury, "naming the game" allows us to convey,

> "Look, I know this may be unusual, but I want to
> know the rules of the game we are going to play.
> Are we both trying to reach a wise agreement as
> quickly and with as little effort as possible? Or are
> we going to play 'hard bargaining' where the more
> stubborn fellow wins?"[7]

Our interest and commitment, of course, is to the
former. We invite them to a different kind of "game."

A Final Thought:
Consider Your Alternative

Not all problems can be solved in a way that will feel
fair and meet the interests of both parties. In the 1980s,
negotiation scholar Howard Raiffa popularized the
term ZOPA, or Zone of Possible Agreement,[8] to refer
to that space where the interests of two parties overlap. This is the space in which a sensible, sustainable
agreement can be had. But not all situations will have
a ZOPA.

There are going to be times when you really need a salary of at least $50,000 and the ministry site can really only afford $30,000. Times when you need the hall on Saturday night and only Friday is available. Times when the job requires nighttime on-call and you can't leave your small children. Sometimes out of a sense of loyalty or obligation or simply a desire to make things work, we bend ourselves into pretzels looking for a configuration that will make both sides happy, but such a configuration doesn't exist.

Inability to find a ZOPA doesn't mean that one or the other of the parties is evil or uncompromising. It doesn't mean they are lying or trying to be unfair. It just means that there isn't enough of an overlap of interests to arrive at an agreement that makes sense for both sides, and—truly—the only kinds of agreements we want to make are those that make sense for both parties. These are the only kinds of agreements that convey a concern for the relationship involved and the only kind that last.

In this case, the best thing to do is to move to what Fisher and Ury term your BATNA, or Best Alternative to a Negotiated Agreement.[9] Distinct from "options"—which are the various possibilities that you try to come up with to meet each other's interests—your BATNA is what you will do if you can't arrive at an agreement. It is what you will do if you decide *not* to take the salary offer on the table. What you will do if you *can't* persuade the other to give you the hall on Saturday. What

you will do if you *can't* acquiesce to the new regulations
requiring nighttime on-call.

While you are working on problem solving with
the other, it is wise to be considering simultaneously
your BATNA. Are you also applying to other jobs?
Will you take some time off? Do you have a savings
account to support such a decision? Will you stay at
your current job? Will you look at another hall that has
Saturday's date open? How much will it cost? Will you
cancel the event?

Thinking about your BATNA will strengthen your
efforts to problem solve in two ways. First, when you
are honest about your BATNA, it can keep you from
becoming doctrinaire in your problem solving. To say
"I will only accept jobs offering $50,000" is great—if
you have another job offer on the table aligned with
your expectations. But if you have been unemployed
for a number of months with no other prospects in sight
and creditors looming, it might be more in your interest to accept the offer with the understanding it may
be short-term. Knowing your BATNA can stop you
from ending your problem-solving efforts with another
prematurely.

Second, once you are conscious of your current
BATNA, you can take proactive steps to better it, which
will make you increasingly free when negotiating with
others. The happier you become with your alternative,
the less apt you are to make concessions that are against
your interests. If there is another hall two miles away

that costs $50 more but has the desired date available, you are not going to invest significant time and energy in trying to come up with more options in this present negotiation. Realizing you have a good BATNA can stop you from extending problem-solving efforts with another beyond the point when you should have let them go.

In Jesus's time, many of those to whom he spoke did not have great BATNAs in their lives. Under Roman occupation, their fates seemed largely determined by others and they naturally would feel victims of their circumstances. Roman soldiers, for example, could demand a local person act as a messenger or porter for up to a mile, and the person would have no voice in the matter. The people hated this and became embittered. What is fascinating about Jesus's teaching is that he reinserts human freedom into the matter: "If anyone forces you to go one mile, go also the second mile" (Mt 5:41).

"It may seem that others are doing what they want with you," he is emphasizing, "but they can never take away your power of choice. They say 'one mile,' you say 'No, I'll go two.' They say 'Give me your right cheek,' you say, 'Here's my left as well.' Your life remains yours."

Sometimes in our own lives, our BATNAs might not feel so great either. And in those circumstances, we, too, can feel like victims of forces beyond our control. It's easy to become bitter and experience ourselves as forced into agreements we don't think are fair. But Jesus's teaching reminds us that no one can ever really take away our power of choice. And when we begin to look at our lives in terms of the concept of BATNA, we can begin to feel a greater sense of control: "No one is making me take this agreement; it's just that I've considered my alternatives and I choose this one. Not necessarily for forever, but at least for now. Later, I might choose something different. But I am the one choosing."

And when we do decide to exercise our BATNA, there need not be shame in that decision. ("I feel so selfish for walking away and leaving them to have to begin the interview process all over again.") Nor need there be bitterness. ("I can't believe they wouldn't raise the salary more for me.") Rather, we recognize agreement isn't always possible at this moment in history and that it makes more sense for both parties to pursue other paths. There is a proverb in the African American community: "Every shut-eye ain't sleep and every good-bye ain't gone." Just because we are walking away from an agreement now doesn't mean that our paths won't across again in the future and, when they do, we can be proud of the way we conducted conversations in the past, knowing that being "trustworthy but not trusting" has laid a solid foundation upon which to negotiate anew.

Companion for the Journey:
Mother Théodore Guérin

"You will say now: 'At last you are settled; peace is going to be restored,'" Théodore Guérin wrote to a longtime friend in France. "Wait a moment before chanting the *Te Deum*."[10]

Guérin should have been celebrating a major breakthrough in her ongoing negotiations with the difficult bishop of Vincennes, Célestine de la Hailandière. But she still had her doubts.

Hailandière had recruited Guérin and several other Sisters of Providence from Ruillé-sur-Loir to begin a new teaching congregation in the mission territory of Indiana in 1840. Guérin and the sisters arrived with the expectation that she would lead the group, that the sisters would be able to construct a rule to guide their common life with each other, and that the diocese would give them a suitable plot of land on which they could build a school and begin to support themselves. As soon as they arrived, however, things began to sour.

It turns out that Hailandière had a terrible habit of micromanaging. He insisted on being involved in every decision, big or small, and—as noted in his funeral eulogy—he "brooked not contradiction."[11] A number of the priests of the diocese, including his own vicar general, fled to the diocese of New Orleans rather than continue working with him.

Upon disembarking from the stagecoach in Vincennes, Guérin and the sisters discovered that the bishop planned to locate them on an un-coveted plot of densely forested land, fifty miles from town, aptly named "Saint Mary-of-the-Woods," which he also refused to deed to them until they had an approved rule. But then he would not approve their rule, continuing to insist on tweaks and rewrites. And, perhaps most problematic, he would not allow Guérin any authority as leader of the small congregation. When she travelled to raise money for the school he wanted the sisters to build, he reassigned her sisters. Once, in her absence, he insisted the sisters hold a new leadership election. (The sisters simply elected Guérin again.) When negotiating with a "hard bargainer" such as this, who wouldn't have doubts?

For seven years, Guérin modeled much of what we've talked about in this chapter. She remained respectful and hopeful for progress, while never naïve. Copies of her correspondence throughout this period evidence her clarity communicating to Hailandière the sisters' interests and potential options for going forward. She "named the game" and asked if this was wise. At the same time, she entered into correspondence with other bishops to investigate relocating the sisters to another diocese—in essence, building her BATNA. When Hailandière made attacks on her character, Guérin never returned the insult, treating him as she would *like* to be treated, not as she *was* being treated.

An example of the tone of her communication can be found in this letter of March 1846, sent upon finally receiving approval of the rule but still not being given the deed to the land:

> We dare hope that you will not delay to give us this last proof of your goodwill, which, in putting an end to a state so painful for all, will open to our view a brighter future. . . . However, faithful to the spirit of candor which we have always followed, we must say that . . . your silence, or any reply which would not be the Acts we ask for, could not but be regarded by us, this time, as a formal refusal; in which case we would consider ourselves obliged to take a definitive resolution.[12]

When Guérin finally did receive the deed to a portion of the land in July 1846, her friends wanted to rejoice. The rule had been approved. The sisters had at least some of the promised land. They would not need to move. Surely now all would be well, right? It turns out that Guérin was correct to remain cautious about singing the *Te Deum*.

On her next visit to Vincennes in April 1847, Hailandière launched into a verbal tirade on Guérin. He removed her as superior, dispensed her of her vows, forbid her to stay in the diocese or to communicate with the sisters, and—at least according to oral tradition—excommunicated her. Then, for good measure, he locked her in his office while he went to eat dinner.[13] Finally, the seven-year back-and-forth between them had come to what certainly looked like a definitive resolution.

But sometimes, it seems providence problem solves in ways humans cannot. Before Guérin could pack her bags and leave town, Hailandière received word he had been relieved of his post. Acknowledging his incapacity to run the diocese as he saw fit, the bishop had submitted a letter of resignation, and it had been accepted.

Guérin remained as leader of the Sisters of Providence at Saint Mary-of-the-Woods until her death in 1856. In her perseverance as a missionary and her capacity to hold her own in the protracted multiyear negotiation with Hailandière, the Catholic Church recognized signs of extraordinary holiness and canonized her a saint in 2006.

For Reflection and Prayer

1. Can you think of a time when you were able to respond to and change a pattern of interaction rather than simply react and unconsciously continue the pattern? What did you try to do differently?

2. What messages about doubt have you received in your life as a Christian? What would a healthy understanding of "doubt" look like for you?

3. What are some of the "games" you think you are most likely to fall prey to in your own efforts to problem solve with others? (Either games that you realize you initiate or games others initiate that you unwittingly get sucked into.)

4. What would you hope to be able to emulate of Mother Théodore Guérin in your own life?

Lord, I am careful and rightly so.

Many times in my life I have been stung,

taken advantage of, and treated unfairly.

And while others have had their role in this, I real-
     ize that I have, too.

I have expected others to be watching out for my
     interests

instead of making these interests known myself.

I have swallowed my questions rather than named
     them.

I have settled when I should have walked on.

So, I'm asking you now not to change the world,
     but to change me.

Teach me how to stand up for what I care about,

so that as the years pass, I might not grow bitter
     but peaceful

with the direction of my life

and ever more free to do good.

Amen.

12. Practice Prudence

For everything there is a season. . . .
A time to weep, and a time to laugh;
a time to mourn, and a time to dance. . . .
A time to embrace, and a time to refrain
from embracing.
A time to seek, and a time to lose; . . .
a time to keep silence, and a time to speak.
A time to love, and a time to hate;
a time for war, and a time for peace.

—Selections from Ecclesiastes 3:1–8

At the famed Uffizi Gallery in Florence hang seven arched panels. They were first commissioned in 1469 by the judges of the Tribunale della Mercatanzia—or Merchants Court—to adorn the backs of their courtroom chairs. Each of the paintings depicts a virtue in the form of a woman. The most famous of the seven (possibly because it has best survived the ravages of time) is Piero del Pollaiolo's *Prudence*.

The word prudence often conjures images of Puritan girls intently engaged in needlepoint or bonneted women with pursed lips and scowls on their faces. We associate it with "being a prude," lacking a sense of humor, or being rigid and risk-averse. But del Pollaiolo's painting does not serve the stereotype. In his portrayal, Prudence is an elegant young woman who holds a mirror in her right hand—associating prudence with the ability to see things clearly, to reflect, and to grasp the truth from another angle. In her left hand, she holds a writhing serpent—hardly an image for the timid but rather a classical symbol for wisdom. Del Pollaiolo is trying to convey prudence in its fuller Christian sense: the ability to know "the good" coupled with an ability to figure out concretely how to keep moving in the direction of "the good," even when there are obstacles in the way.

In the course of this book, we've looked at a plethora of practices that we want to have at our disposal in times of tension:

- side-stepping the triangle
- stirring curiosity
- listening toward understanding
- untangling intent and impact
- welcoming emotion
- speaking one's voice
- knowing and steadying oneself
- praying to forgive

- repenting
- problem solving
- testing doubts and alternatives

We could think of each of these practices as a tool in our toolbox. We know a carpenter is only as good as his tools; at the same time, simply possessing good tools does not make one a carpenter. It's a question of knowing which tool to use when and how. Likewise, having a book full of habits doesn't necessarily serve excellence in Christian conflict unless we say something about the art of how these habits work together in the arc of ongoing conversation. "There's an appointed time for everything," says the writer of Ecclesiastes. The challenge is figuring out what is the "appointed time" for what action. In essence, everything we've talked about thus far would remain incomplete without the practice of prudence.

The Foundation of Prudence: Remembering the Ultimate Goal

In Lewis Carroll's fantasy *Alice's Adventures in Wonderland*, there is a scene in which Alice finds herself at a crossroad with multiple potential paths before her. She asks the Cheshire Cat:

> "Would you tell me please which way I ought to walk from here?"

"That depends a good deal on where you want to get to," said the Cat.

"I don't much care . . ." said Alice.

"Then it doesn't matter which way you walk," said the Cat.[1]

To practice prudence first implies ascertaining where you want to go. Until an end is determined, it doesn't help to talk about which practices to engage in which order.

In the opening pages of this book, we noted that ultimately the goal of all Christian living is participation in the Trinitarian life—a share in God's own utterly relational life. To put it another way, "the good" for which we are meant is communion in diversity. Practicing prudence in the midst of conflict means keeping the vision of communion in diversity ever before us. It does not mean that any one conversation is going to get us to our desired destiny, nor does it mean there is only one way to get there. But it does mean making sure our choices about next steps are in step with the end we want.

Because communion in diversity is the most elevated of potential destinations, the journey toward it is going to naturally require more exertion than other destinations. We will need to take breaks in the conversation along the way. We may need to put some relationships on hold for a while. As discussed in chapter 8, there are even relationships we might need to put on hold indefinitely this side of death. But we don't let go of the final destination. I've heard people say before, "I don't have to deal with this situation because I never plan on having anything to do with this person again in my lifetime," and, indeed, sometimes that might be the right approach to take, just so long as one recognizes that from a Christian point of view, there is yet more road on the other side of death.

If the Christian intuition about the profound mercy of God is correct, chances are I will be living with those I don't like, those who cause me grief, or those I consider "enemy" for all of eternity. If *I* were God, I would have in mind another destination for my enemies. But—luckily for some—I am not God and have no say in the matter. And so, God gives me a choice: I can move in the direction of working things out on this side of the grave or I can move in the direction of working them out on the other side of the grave, but either way, eventually they'll have to get worked out. Heaven, by definition, *won't be heaven for me* unless I have fully actualized my capacity for living communion in diversity.

Hence, when tempted to turn my gaze toward other attractive destination points for a difficult conversation—like teaching them a lesson, venting my anger and hurt, exacting just a bit of revenge, or simply hands-down "winning"—prudence reminds me that, even though the alternatives are much easier to reach, I could find myself seated next to my "enemy" in the heavenly court for longer than the sun will continue to shine. I want to make sure that whatever step I take next will somehow make sense in that *very* big, *very* long-range picture.

Reflecting from Another Angle

With our gaze fixed on eternity, how do we leap into the conversations we find tough now? In chapter 2, we talked about three manageable purposes for a fruitful if difficult conversation: learning more information, sharing our perspective, and problem solving. But how do we make sure from the start that the conversation heads in this direction?

Often we jump into a tough conversation through the angle of our own perspective. ("Can we talk about why you guys are so unwilling to compromise on the use of the parish hall?") Sometimes, in an effort to be magnanimous, we might try to go into the conversation from their angle. ("So how do you think things are going between our two groups right now?") Neither one of these angles is particularly successful for beginning a conversation where there is tension. The first can immediately trigger defensiveness on the other's part. The second often triggers suspicion that we are trying to trap them or simply pretending to be curious before inserting our own version of the story.

Note that in del Pollaiolo's painting, Prudence holds her mirror at such an angle that she can see what she looks like—and what her surroundings look like—from an outsider's point of view. Likewise, the most productive angle from which to enter a tough conversation is what we might call the "outside angle."[2] It is the angle that a mediator or counselor would take in giving a synopsis of what is going on from an objective, outsider's perspective. It is the type of description you might see captured in a newspaper headline or described by a disinterested observer to the action.

- "The Boy Scout troop and the food pantry volunteers are both interested in using the parish hall at the same time."

- "Mrs. Garcia, the last time we talked, you and I expressed a difference of opinion about the best date and timing of your daughter Ada's upcoming quinceañera celebration."

Initiating the conversation from this angle allows one to name the purposes of the conversation upfront and set it on the right path without raising the other's defenses or suspicions.

- "Let's you and I talk more to understand what's at stake for both groups in this decision about space and see what kinds of options might make the most sense."

- "Mrs. Garcia, I want to understand better why scheduling the event sooner is important to you and what is going on behind the scenes on your side. I also want to share with you more about what it means to me as the staff member who coordinates all quinceañeras. And I want to see if we can figure out a solution that will work for both of us. I don't know what that is yet; maybe there isn't one. But I want to try."

Note that if the other person is the one to initiate the conversation, even unexpectedly, you can still reframe their opening to the outsider's angle.

Mrs. Garcia: "I don't understand why you are making it so difficult for Ada to do her quinceañera here at the parish."

Parish Ministry Coordinator: "Mrs. Garcia, it sounds like you and I are both experiencing a lot of frustration around the scheduling of this event, which seems like it shouldn't be this difficult—probably to both of us. Help me understand why this date is important and what is happening on your side, and then I'd like to share the constraints we're under and some of the dilemmas I face. I'd like to see if we can find a solution that will work for both of us."

Even if they start inside their own perspective, you can broaden the frame to include both stories as important parts of working it out together.

As Agile as the Serpent

In preparing to have a conversation that you find difficult to engage, it helps to think about how you want to start. You might even want to script out your opening sentences. (I know I do!) But once you name your purposes, the conversation will inevitably move into unscripted territory. While it makes sense to have a few questions in mind that you want to make sure you ask, it will not help to write down in advance how you want the conversation to go. The other person will never play his or her part as you have scripted it in your mind. Because you'll be waiting for a cue for your own lines (which will rarely come), you will have a hard time listening to what the other person actually does say.

Instead, hold onto the age-old symbol of Prudence's serpent as a creature that can move around obstacles and bend and be flexible, easily wiggling into small open spaces in the conversation to explore them further. There is no particular order that the conversation has to move through in order to accomplish its purposes. Often, it works well to begin by listening to the other person first to make sure you understand well his or her perspective. Often, it makes sense to hold off on problem-solving mode for a while before you have acquired some additional information about what is at stake for the other party and what that person's real interests are. But many times you will find that the conversation jumps around quite a bit and there is no one right way to do it so long as you are aiming in the direction of communion in diversity. For example:

When They Convey . . .	Potential Ways to Keep Moving Forward
"You aren't listening to what I am saying."	"Let me say what I think I've heard you say and then you tell me what you think I'm missing." **(Listening toward Understanding)**
	"I admit I'm having a hard time because when you talk it's also triggering a lot in me. It would help if I could say a bit about what's going on in my mind." **(Speak Your Voice)**
"You ask for input but then you never take it."	"That's hard to hear. I like to think of myself as collaborative. Could you give me an example of a time when you saw me do that?" **(Knowing and Steadying Oneself)**
	"Ah, that's interesting. So it sounds like when I ask for input but then move in a different direction, you wonder whether I heard you or took your input seriously. In fact, the input I've gotten from you and others has been invaluable. But it sounds like I haven't done a very good job of sharing that or, when I don't follow the suggestions you've offered, why. My intent is to be both inclusive and decisive, but it sounds like that is not how I'm coming across." **(Untangling Knot of Intent and Impact)**

When They Convey . . .	Potential Ways to Keep Moving Forward
"Come on, we always do it your way. It's time you compromise and do it my way."	"It sounds like the way we've been making decisions as a team has been pretty frustrating to you and maybe feels like it hasn't been fair." **(Welcoming Emotion)** "We could make this a contest of wills, but I'm not sure that is the best way to make a decision on something as important as this. I guess what would persuade me to try your suggestion would be if you could explain . . ." **(Testing Doubts and Alternatives)** "I am sorry. I have been pretty insistent on some things lately that were important to me and it sounds like this is important to you." **(Repenting)**
"This conversation is over."	"Maybe you've said all the things that you'd hoped to say. But there are a couple of things I'd like to still get out on the table, whether we talk about them now or tomorrow." **(Speaking Your Voice)** "This seems to be a pattern in how we end arguments with each other—you deciding the conversation is over and me acquiescing. I don't think it's serving our relationship well, and I'd like to come up with another way to resolve our disagreements." **(Testing Doubts and Alternatives)**

When They Convey . . .	Potential Ways to Keep Moving Forward
"I said I was sorry; when are you going to get over this?"	"I admit I'm holding onto some stuff from the past. When you say that, though, I feel judged and misunderstood, and I think it actually slows down my ability to let it go." **(Praying to Forgive)** "I guess I'm uneasy. I heard the 'sorry' and at the same time, I've not seen a change in attitude or behavior that would tell me it won't happen again. 　　What would help me get over this is believing you really understand the impact it has had on me and hearing you talk about what you'd do differently in the future." **(Testing Doubts and Alternatives)** "You sound frustrated that this event from our past is still coming up in conversation." **(Welcoming Emotion)**

Walking the Winding Road

This book has been filled with short snippets of conversations—conversations going wrong but also lots of conversations beginning to go right. Let's flesh out two of those conversations a little more to see how by engaging prudence some of the various practices we've looked at in previous chapters could be interlaced to move the conversation in the promising direction of communion, even in the midst of real differences of perspective.

> *Chaplain*: Gordon, last week you and I had a conversation about the director of pastoral care position. You let me know that you'd decided to appoint Xavier to the position rather than me. That was kind of a rough day for me and I wanted the chance just to talk about the decision more—to ask some questions about it, and also to see if there is anything more you wanted to say to me about it that I wasn't able to hear when I first found out. **(Starting from the Outsider's Angle/ Establishing Purposes)**

> *VP of Mission*: Sure, though I thought I explained last week that Xavier simply had more CPE units than you and just seemed like the right fit for what the role needs at this point in time.

> *Chaplain*: Well, I guess this is what confuses me. I do realize that he has more CPE units, though the job description only listed the requirement of four, which we both have. So I'm more intrigued by your statement about

"fit"—what do you mean by that? **(Listening toward Understanding)**

VP of Mission: In the five years that Xavier has been here, he has done a lot to build rapport with not only the other chaplains but also with the nursing staff and even physicians. I think he'll be a prominent personality to elevate the role of the chaplaincy department within the hospital.

Chaplain: I've long appreciated Xavier's friendliness myself. Is that what really stood out to you in terms of fit, or were there other things? **(Listening toward Understanding)**

VP of Mission: No, that's it.

Chaplain: I have something tugging in the back of my mind that I rather wish would go quiet, but throughout this past week, it hasn't—so I just want to raise it with you and ask about it. What I'm wondering is whether "fit" didn't also have to do with the fact that he's a man and I'm a woman? **(Untangling Knot of Intent and Impact/Testing Doubts and Alternatives)**

VP of Mission: What are you insinuating?

Chaplain: Nothing, I hope. I'm trying to be transparent about assumptions that are running through my mind so that I don't keep going on thinking them if they aren't based in reality. I think if I didn't get a chance to talk about this directly with you, it might sour our working relationship with each other in the future, and I don't want that. **(Untangling Knot of Intent and Impact/Sidestepping the Triangle)**

VP of Mission: Well, I appreciate that, but what are you basing this crazy idea on?

Chaplain: Well, the three people who've held this position since I've been here the last twelve years have all been men. Of the thirty directors at the hospital right now, fewer than a third of them are women. None of the senior executives are women, save the Chief Nursing Officer. From where I sit, that data really leaps out to me, and I tend to think that it influences decisions about who gets promoted to leadership or not. **(Speaking Your Voice)**

VP of Mission: But that's just not true.

Chaplain: Tell me about how you see it differently. What do you think I should be paying attention to that I'm not? **(Listening toward Understanding)**

VP of Mission: That 40 percent of our patient population now is Spanish-speaking, and Xavier is fluent in Spanish. That even though we have few women in leadership, we have even fewer persons of color. And that is something that I think we also really need to be looking at as an institution. . . . And, as I said, Xavier has fostered a great relationship with the wider staff.

Chaplain: I actually share an interest in a diverse leadership team in terms of both gender and ethnicity. I'm not opposed to you there. I also care about this. **(Problem Solving by Separating Interests from Positions)** I need to better understand your last statement though about Xavier's great relationship with the staff. Do you mean to say his relationships are better than mine? **(Listening toward Understanding)**

VP of Mission: Well, I didn't say that, but I guess I *would* say that. I think the staff experiences you as—well, how would I say this?—rather "strident."

Chaplain: Wow. Could you say some more about what you've heard or seen that comes off as "strident"? **(Listening toward Understanding)**

VP of Mission: Well, in meetings, you speak very confidently about what would be "just" and what the "right thing to do" would be. I believe in justice and doing the right thing, too, but the way you talk, it doesn't seem to leave room for anyone to express another opinion. It leads to others in the room being afraid to speak up or ask questions. Health care is super-complicated, and sometimes I think you see it from just one angle.

Chaplain: I'm not trying to come off as defensive; I really want to make sure I am understanding what you are seeing. Could you give me an example of a time when I came across as strident in a meeting? **(Knowing and Steadying Oneself)**

VP of Mission: I'd have to think about it some . . . well, okay, here's one: the meeting with Xavier, Donna, and me a couple of weeks ago. We were all planning Peter's going-away party, and you had really strong ideas about how we were obligated as a hospital to honor his service as director of pastoral care in such-and-such a way. You kept stressing that it was the right thing to do, as if other suggestions were inherently wrong. And short of unceremoniously kicking Peter out on his rear, it seems to me there was a wide range of ways we could honor his service. It just wasn't so black and white.

Chaplain: Huh. That certainly wasn't my intent. I wanted Peter to know how much we loved him and would miss him, but I didn't know I was coming off as dictatorial. I mean, it gives me something to think about. **(Untangling Knot of Intent and Impact)** Gordon, this has been helpful to me. You've clarified a couple of things that were really troubling to me and also gave me some new things to think about. I'm not sure what to do with it all yet, but if I do have more questions, I'm trusting it is okay to come back and talk some more.

VP of Mission: Of course. I'm glad you raised it with me.

Professor: I was surprised to see your name on the class roster again this semester.

Student: Yeah, my advisor told me that I needed to give you a second chance . . . and your class was the only one that fit in my course schedule.

Professor: I know we had a real difference of opinion about grades at the end of last semester and I'm guessing neither of us wants a repeat of that scenario, so I wanted to touch base with you before the semester began to see if we could start again on a better note. **(Starting from the Outsider's Angle/Establishing Purposes)**

Student: Well . . . thanks.

Professor: If I remember right, last time you felt like I shorted the time I spent with your group and that you didn't get the attention from me that would have benefited your learning. **(Listening toward Understanding)**

Student: That's true.

Professor: I'm stuck in a somewhat similar situation this semester in that I have a large group and no teaching assistant to help with grading. It's hard for me to have a lot of individualized time with students and, at the same time, I really do want each student to feel like he or she is being graded fairly. From where you sit, what kinds of things might I do differently this semester that would let students know I, too, value fairness? **(Listening toward Understanding/Problem Solving)**

Student: Well, if there are going to be group projects again, maybe instead of meeting with each group during class time to explain the assignment, you could have groups come to you during office hours so that there wouldn't be so much time pressure and each group could have the time it needs with you.

Professor: That wouldn't be hard to do. Let me ask though: As a student, do you think that groups would be able to manage setting up a separate time to come see me outside class time? Or is that going to be hard for them to coordinate? **(Problem Solving)**

Student: No, I think it would be doable.

Professor: That's an idea worth thinking about as I finalize the syllabus. I'll ask a couple other students what they think about this, too, to get broader feedback. There's one thing I want to ask of you also as we go at this anew. **(Speaking Your Voice)**

Student: What is it?

Professor: If you are offended by something I say or do in the class, can you come talk to me about it when it happens instead of waiting till the end of the semester or bringing the dean into the conversation? I like finding out about problems while there is still time to fix them rather than after the semester is over. **(Sidestepping the Triangle)**

Student: Yes, I can do that.

Professor: Out of curiosity, why didn't you come see me last semester when you started to feel unfairly treated? **(Listening toward Understanding)**

Student: Well, you always seem busy and frazzled. You didn't seem interested in what individual student needs might be. I didn't want to bother you.

Professor: It's true that I am busy and frazzled, and I can see now how that is contributing to the larger problem because I'm probably unintentionally sending mixed messages about my approachability. **(Repenting)** I have a heavier teaching and advising load now than I've ever had before. But I am also very interested in individual students and what would help their learning best. I need students like yourself to really make me aware of your needs explicitly because I am so busy I might not notice. **(Speaking Your Voice)**

Student: I can do that.

Professor: Maybe pop by my office during office hours once every other week and let me know where you are at with the course? **(Problem Solving)**

Student: Yup. I will.

Professor: Do you have any other suggestions for me for how I can let students know that their individual concerns really are a priority?

Student: Let me think about that. I'll get back to you.

When in Doubt . . .

No matter how flexible and experienced you are in the art of Christian conflict, you will have times in the conversation that take your breath away. Times when you freeze up. Times when you are so triggered or so shocked or so undone or so angry that you just can't imagine what to say or do next. And, no matter how "prudential" you become, these times aren't going to go away.

So if all of the practices of this book flee from your memory in the moment of tension, if all of your well-crafted phrases evaporate and your carefully prepared questions are nowhere to be found, remember this: you can't go wrong by leaning in and saying, "Tell me more." And perhaps this is why, in del Pollaiolo's painting, Prudence's mouth is at rest. There is a time for everything under the sun, but when in doubt, Prudence knows it is always the right time to listen.

Companion for the Journey: **Prudence Crandall**

"Miss Crandall, I want to get a little more learning. If possible, enough to teach colored children, and if you will admit me to your school, I shall forever be under greatest obligation to you. If you think it will be the means of injuring you, I will not insist on the favor."[3]

The letter came from a twenty-year-old African American woman named Sarah Harris, and it touched an educator's heart. The aptly-named Prudence Crandall, a Quaker teacher not much older than Harris, had opened a private academy for girls in Canterbury, Connecticut, only a year earlier in 1832. And, although it had not originally been her intent to launch the first integrated classroom in the history of the United States,

that is exactly what she did in early 1833 when she
welcomed Harris into the student body.

Word of Harris's admission triggered a strong,
negative response from the parents of the other students, many of whom threatened to remove their
daughters from the school immediately if Harris was
not dismissed. Crandall was in a difficult situation. She
had invested all of her property and accumulated significant debt in the creation of this school. Nevertheless,
abolitionist attorney Samuel May (a relative of Louisa
May Alcott) recalls upon meeting her,

> Though beat upon by such a storm, we found Miss
> Crandall resolved and tranquil. The effect of her
> Quaker discipline appeared in every word she
> spoke, and in every expression of her countenance.
> . . . She could not make up her mind to comply
> with such a demand, even to save the institution
> she had so recently established with such fond
> hopes. . . . She determined to act right, and leave
> the event with God.[4]

Crandall approached other African American families along the East Coast about sending their daughters
to the school. Before the start of the next semester, she
had transformed her school into an academy solely for
girls of color.

Rather than calming the local citizens, however,
Prudence's decision to restructure and remain open
inflamed them further. Crandall's students were

harassed by townsfolk who pelted them with eggs and manure. The school's well was contaminated. Nearby shopkeepers refused to sell the school necessary food and supplies. The local church refused access to worship services. Before summer arrived, town leaders had persuaded the Connecticut legislature to enact the "black laws" forbidding schools within the state to teach African Americans from outside the state.

Now facing legal consequences, Crandall still decided to carry on with her school. She was arrested and forced to endure a lengthy trial that went on for several months before being dismissed on a technicality. Then, in early September 1834, a nighttime attempt was made to burn down the school, where Crandall boarded with the girls. Luckily, the fire did not catch and Crandall kept the school in session, thinking that the potentially murderous intent of the act would awaken the local community to say "enough is enough." Instead, on September 9, a band of men attacked the house with iron bars, breaking ninety windowpanes.

The next day, Crandall, together with May, called together the students and let them know that they were closing the school. "The words," recalled May, "almost blistered on my lips,"[5] but by that point in time, the "greatest good" seemed to be the girls' immediate safety and prudence meant shuttering the doors.

In spring of 1835, Crandall—now thirty-one years old—put her house on the market and left Connecticut, never to return. "Very true I thought many of the high-minded worldly men would oppose the plan but that Christians would act so unwisely and conduct [themselves] in a manner so outrageously was a thought distant from my view," she wrote in one of her letters, but, "I have put my hand to the plough and I will never no never look back."[6]

Crandall continued teaching and acting on behalf of social justice into her old age. She travelled widely as a public speaker on behalf of voting rights and tolerance. In 1886, 112 citizens of Canterbury signed a petition expressing remorse for how they had treated her and asking that she receive a state pension—a request that was granted by the state legislature. Mark Twain, then a resident of Connecticut, led a movement to buy back her Canterbury home. Crandall's original school building is now the Prudence Crandall museum—an ongoing testimony to the twenty brave young African American women and their principal who demonstrated the many faces of prudence in a discouraging and dangerous conflict.

For Reflection and Prayer

1. Piero del Pollaiolo imaged prudence as a woman carrying a mirror and a serpent. If you were to create an image of prudence, what would you

include as symbols of what is required to practice this virtue?

2.   When considering the relationship you find most challenging right now, is it helpful or unhelpful to imagine yourself sitting next to that person for all of eternity? Does imagining eternity in this fashion change your thinking at all about what the "next step" in your communication with this person might be?

3.   What do you make of the idea to use "listening" as a default practice when you are not quite sure what to do in a conversation? Are there qualifications you would want to add to this advice?

4.   How does Prudence Crandall's simultaneous flexibility and persistence speak to you in your own life?

Most Holy Trinity, for reasons I will never fully
    understand,
you created me with the intent that for all eternity
    I share in your life
—an ongoing dance of communion in diversity
that bursts the boundaries of time.
The very thought fills me with wonder and awe,
but it also fills me with trepidation.

For it is an invitation you have issued not to me
     alone,
but to all of humanity.
When I look at the world around me,
I simply do not know how we are going to get
     there.
I know my destiny is tied up with theirs and theirs
     with mine,
but I think we are going to need a lot of help here.
As I commit myself anew to walk in your light and
     toward your light,
I ask for an abundance of prudence—that I might
     not lose hope,
but instead possess all the creativity and persever-
     ance needed
to live up to this marvelous divine vocation.
Show me now the next step to take.
One step closer to your dream.
Amen.

Conclusion

What you do matters—but not much.
What you are matters tremendously.

—Catherine de Hueck-Doherty

A few years ago now, I picked up my cousin at the airport to bring her to her childhood home where her dad was dying of cancer. The illness had progressed to the stage where it frustrated those of us in the family with Saint Martha genes: Can't we bring more food? More prayers? More fuzzy blankets? But, no, the freezer, the linen closet, and even the "spiritual bouquet" shelf were well-stocked.

When my cousin entered the house, she walked directly into the bedroom and said, "Is there anything you need, Dad?" and he simply pointed to the space next to him in bed. She lay down at his side and put her head on his shoulder. "Closer," he said. She scooted in more. "Closer," he said again. "I can't," she stated, "or I'd hurt you." "I'd be okay with that," he whispered.

I've thought about that moment hundreds of times now. In the end, we don't want blankets and food, maybe not even prayers. What we want is those we love close to us. So close to us that they become one with us. The deepest human desire is not for stuff but for communion. We are wired to love and to be loved.

Is it really any surprise that Jesus would express this desire himself on the night before he died? There were no more trips to the temple to take. No more fishing expeditions on the Sea of Galilee to be had. No more calling and following and inviting, "Come!" His last request, his deepest desire, as expressed in the Gospel of John, was that we simply remain with him and in him.

It seems like such a simple thing to do—just remain? That is all you want of me—just to be with you? Rest with you? Not serve you? Not make great sacrifices for you? Not move mountains for you? Just remain with you?

Simple indeed, until you try it. At which point, we discover that *remaining* is perhaps the most difficult of activities humans ever undertake.

Often remaining is a most pleasurable activity— sitting with those we love and spending time with them. But remaining also requires the capacity to still be there after they've told the same story umpteen times and their quaint little patterns of speech have become grating. And sometimes remaining requires staying in the same room when you are so angry with them you could spit. It means continuing to talk and to share your feelings even when they are ugly and tangled and it'd be easier to create a wall of silence twelve feet thick. And then sometimes—as I saw with my cousin and uncle—remaining means you will see people you love in tremendous pain and that is *such* an uncomfortable place to be. Or it means *being seen* in all one's weakness and vulnerability and need, which for some of us is probably the hardest of all.

We often talk as if "going" requires the greatest strength. We admire those who run marathons and travel to faraway, exotic places—sacrificing life and limb to conquer the frontiers of human capacity. But, perhaps in the end, the greater strength is manifest not in our going but in our remaining—with Lucy in her addiction problem, with the husband who paints the kitchen Big Bird yellow, with the church beautifica-tion committee in its budget debate, with Mrs. Garcia and her demanding calendar, with a loved one on his deathbed.

Yet while we readily acknowledge the skill and practice it takes to keep moving when others would be inclined to give up, we rarely give more than lip service to the immense skill and practice it takes to remain when others would be inclined to move on. When I first began studying and trying to practice a different way of doing conflict in my own setting many moons ago, I thought that if my community learned a few new ideas and vocabulary, we'd be able to solve our issues with one another once and for all: we would enjoy conflict resolution. That did not happen; it still hasn't happened. Rather, conflict continues to flourish among us. But what the skills and long practice have offered is the ability to *remain* in ever-deepening relationship with each other, even when we don't agree. It turns out redeeming conflict is not about *fixing* conflict but managing it in such a way that we rob it of the power to divide and fragment while heightening its power to educate and illumine. *Redeeming* conflict is about becoming more happy, healthy, truthful, and free in our relationships even while it's not all figured out. It is lifelong work.

Not long ago, my friend's seven-year-old daughter walked into the kitchen while my friend was wiping off the countertops and conversing with her husband. Her daughter stood there for a moment akimbo, and then declared, "So . . . *this* is life. I thought it would have more pizzazz." She then departed the room.

The words had a certain hilarity to them coming from a seven-year-old, but they capture a reality that dawns on each of us at one time or another: So *this* is life. This being with one another. This listening to one another. This making decisions with one another. This saying "I'm sorry." This forgiving one another and seeking to understand. *This* is life. And while it is at times a slow slog and lacks "pizzazz," it is a rich life. It is a deep life. It is a partaking in the Trinitarian life. It is a taste of eternal life; a taste of heaven.

Notes

1. Sidestep the Triangle

1. One example of where this language is used is Ted Dunn, "Triangulation and the Misuse of Power," *Human Development* 27, no. 1 (2006): 18–26.

2. Ibid., 23.

3. Ibid., 23.

4. Prosper of Aquitaine, quoted in *Readings in European History*, trans. J. H. Robinson (Boston: Ginn, 1905), 49–51.

2. Be Curious

1. See for example Eph 1:13, Col 1:5, and Jas 1:18.

2. 1 Cor 13:6 and Jn 3:21, respectively.

3. Jn 14:6.

4. 1 Jn 5:6.

5. Thomas Aquinas, *Summa Theologica*, part I, question 16, article 1, vol. 1 (Allen, TX: Christian Classics, 1948), 89–90.

6. Ludwig Wittgenstein, *On Certainty*, trans. G. E. M. Anscombe and G. H. von Wright (New York: Harper, 1972), 245. Quoted in Scott Steinkerchner, *Beyond Agreement: Interreligious Dialogue Amid Persistent Differences* (New York: Rowman & Littlefield, 2010), 42.

7. I want to thank former colleague Dominic Holtz, O.P., for this image.

8. This concept has a long history within Christianity and could be attributed to a number of sources, most recently including Benedict XVI, "Christmas Address 2012," in *Commonweal*, August 15, 2014, edition.

9. Zora Neale Hurston, *Their Eyes Were Watching God* (Champaign, IL: University of Illinois Press, 1991), 27.

10. The term "learning conversation" is used by Douglas Stone, Bruce Patton, and Sheila Heen in *Difficult Conversations: How to Discuss*

What Matters Most (New York: Penguin, 2010). See especially its introduction on pages 18–19.

11. Many insights from this chapter—including the three purposes of difficult conversation—have been gleaned from Stone, Patton, and Heen, *Difficult Conversations*, especially chapters 2 and 7.

3. Listen toward Understanding

1. Walter Brueggemann, *Genesis: Interpretation: A Bible Commentary for Teaching and Preaching* (Westminster: John Knox, 1982), 97–105.

2. Ibid. On page 103, Brueggemann notes the number of times that "hear" or "ears" is mentioned in Acts 2, including vv. 6, 8, 11, 14, and 37.

3. Ibid., 104.

4. It is hard to find Argyris's initial reference to the ladder, but his understanding is clearly described in Chris Argyris, *Overcoming Organizational Defenses: Facilitating Organizational Learning* (Boston: Allyn and Bacon, 1990).

5. Stephen R. Covey, *The Seven Habits of Highly Effective People: Restoring the Character Ethic* (New York: Simon and Schuster, 1989), 241.

6. Paul Moses, *The Saint and the Sultan* (New York: Doubleday, 2009), 50ff.

7. For a mix of opinions about Francis's motives, see John Tolan, *Saint Francis and the Sultan* (Oxford University Press, 2009), 6–7, as well as Moses, *The Saint and the Sultan*, 6.

8. Tolan, *Saint Francis and the Sultan*, 5–6.

9. Jacques de Vitry, *Historia occidentalis* (ca. 1223) quoted in John Tolan, *Saint Francis and the Sultan*, 20. A bas relief depicting the event outside Saint Joseph Church in Cairo, Egypt, portrays the sultan as leaning forward in his throne, giving Francis his utmost attention. The 1909 bas relief sculpture by Arnoldo Zocchi is described and photographed in Moses's book *The Saint and the Sultan*, 236.

10. Ibid., 20.

11. See Francis's "Letter to the Custodians," "Letter to the Rulers of the People," and his "Letter to the Entire Order"—quoted in Kathleen

Warren, OSF, *Resource Materials for the Footprints of Francis and the Sultan: A Model for Peacemaking* (Cincinnati, OH: Franciscan Media, 2013), 34.

12. Ibid., 34.

13. This story appears in multiple places online (e.g., see http://darvish.wordpress.com/2008/12/23/st-francis-meets-sultan-malik-al-kamil/), but I was not able to find an original source for it.

4. Undo the Knot of Intention

1. Pope Francis, "Address on 'The Faith of Mary,'" *vatican.va*, October 12, 2013, http://www.news.va/en/news/pope-francis-speaks-about-the-faith-of-mary.

2. Stone, Patton, and Heen, *Difficult Conversations* 46–47.

3. Ibid., 47–48.

4. For a fine synthesis of current research on the impact of emotion on memory and learning, see Celeste DeSchryver Mueller, "To Be Leaven: Transformational Teaching Practices in the Formation of Mission Leaders" (DMin thesis, Eden Theological Seminary, 2006.)

5. This is a commonly used quote of uncertain origin. This was the most aged source I could find, but it may have other roots. Accessed at http://forward.com/articles/128487/religion-within-the-bounds-of-reason-and-love/#ixzz3K7VBfYbg.

6. Aquinas, *Summa Theologica*, I–II.8.1, vol. 2, 626–627. Emphasis added.

7. Quoted in Marie-Patricia Burns, V.H.M., *Friendship, Forgiveness, and the Founders of the Salesian* Tradition (New York: De Sales Resource Center, 2009).

8. Ibid.

5. Welcome Emotion

1. Rumi, "The Guest House," in *The Essential Rumi*, trans. Coleman Barks with John Moyne (New York: Harper San Francisco, 1995), 109.

2. Paul Ekman, "Basic Emotions," in *The Handbook of Cognition and Emotion*, eds. T. Dalgeish and T. Power, (Sussex, UK: John Wiley & Sons, 1999), 45–60.

3. For a stunning example of this, listen to the "Overcome by Emotion" episode of RadioLab, http://www.radiolab.org/story/91642-overcome-by-emotion/, reporting Antoine Bechara's research related to a man who, after surgery for a brain tumor, lost his capacity for feeling and its impact on his decision-making capacities.

4. For more information on Fisher and Shapiro's research and recommendations on the core emotional concerns see Roger Fisher and Daniel Shapiro, *Beyond Reason* (New York: Viking, 2005).

5. Ibid., 21.

6. Ibid., 215–216.

7. Douglas Stone and Sheila Heen, *Thanks for the Feedback* (New York: Penguin, 2013), 150–154. Stone and Heen base the percentage noted on work done by Richard J. Davidson, *The Emotional Life of Your Brain: How Its Unique Patterns Affect the Way You Think, Feel, and Live—and How You Can Change Them* (New York: Hudson Street Press, 2002), 41, 69.

8. For a fuller discussion of how to work with feelings in a difficult conversation, see Stone, Patton, and Heen, *Difficult Conversations* chapter 5.

9. Augustine of Hippo, *Confessions*, III.

10. Ibid.

11. Augustine of Hippo, *Confessions*, X.

12. Augustine of Hippo, *Confessions*, III 11(19).

6. Speak Your Voice

1. Charlotte Linde, quoted in Deborah Tannen, "How to Give Orders Like a Man," *New York Times Magazine* 143 (August 28, 1994): 46.

2. Charlotte Linde, "The Quantitative Study of Communicative Success: Politeness and Accidents in Aviation Discourse," *Language in Society* 17 (1988): 375–399.

3. Quoted in Deborah Tannen, "How to Give Orders Like a Man," *New York Times Magazine* 143 (August 28, 1994): 46.

4. Amy Cuddy, "Your Body Language Shapes Who You Are," TED Global, recorded June 2012. Available at www.ted.com.

5. Eric H. F. Law, *The Wolf Shall Dwell with the Lamb: A Spirituality for Leadership in a Multicultural Community* (Saint Louis, MO: Chalice Press, 1993), 81ff.

6. Ibid., 83–85.

7. "The Acts of Paul and Thekla" can be found in numerous publications and online. One site with an easy-to-read English translation is http://legacy.fordham.edu/halsall/basis/thecla.asp.

7. Know and Steady Thyself

1. For one instance of where this appears in his writing, see Augustine of Hippo, *Soliloquies* II, 1, 1. Fuller quote: "*Deus semper idem, noverim me, noverim te. Oratum est*—God, You who are always the same, here I am, I would like to know myself and, alike, to know You. This is my prayer."

2. Augustinians of the Assumption, "The Art of Discernment According to Saint Augustine," *Itinéraires augustiniens*, vol. 36, trans. Fr. Joseph Fredette, A.A., available at www.augnet.org.

3. Stone and Heen, *Thanks for the Feedback*, 8.

4. Ibid.

5. Ibid., 48ff.

6. Augustine of Hippo, *Confessions*, 10, 13, trans. Gary Wills, *Saint Augustine: A Life* (New York: Penguin, 1999), 89.

7. Brad A. Binau, "Administrative Ministry: A Link Between Shame and Stress," *Trinity Seminary Review* 27, no. 2, (Summer–Fall 2006): 100–101.

8. Stone and Heen, *Thanks for the Feedback*, 161ff.

9. Augustine of Hippo, *Confessions*, 10.

10. Augustine of Hippo, *De Diversis*, 83. 71. 5.

11. Parker Palmer, *A Hidden Wholeness* (San Francisco: Jossey-Bass, 2004), 58–59.

12. Ibid.

13. Salvador Carranza, "The Reluctant Conversion of Oscar Romero," *Sojourners*, (March–April 2000).

14. Thomas M. Kelly, *When the Gospel Grows Feet: Rutilio Grande, SJ, and the Church of El Salvador* (Collegeville, MN: Liturgical Press, 2013).

15. Rutilio Grande, S.J., "Homily preached February 13, 1977," available at http://cjd.org/2012/07/08/monsenor-the-last-journey-of-oscar-romero/#sthash.T33PxadH.dpuf.

16. Juan Macho, "The Reluctant Conversion of Oscar Romero," *Sojourners*, (March–April 2000).

17. Delfin W. Bautista, "Lenten Friendship: Reflecting on the Life of Oscar Romero," available at http://www.believeoutloud com/latest/lenten-friendship-reflecting-life-oscar-romero.

18. Oscar Romero, "Funeral Homily for Rutilio Grande," March 14, 1977.

19. Inocencio Alas, "The Reluctant Conversion of Oscar Romero," *Sojourners*, (March–April 2000).

8. Pray to Forgive

1. Everett L. Worthington, Charlotte Van Oyen Witvliet, Pietro Pietrini, and Andrea J. Miller, "Forgiveness, Health, and Well-Being: A Review of Evidence for Emotional Versus Decisional Forgiveness, Dispositional Forgiveness, and Reduced Unforgiveness," *Journal of Behavioral Medicine* 30, no. 4 (August 2007): 291–302. See also Fredric Luskin, *Forgive for Good* (San Francisco: Harper, 2002).

2. Bruce Malina, *The New Testament World: Insights from Cultural Anthropology* (Atlanta: John Knox Press, 1981), 25–50.

3. Marie M. Fortune, "Preaching Forgiveness?" in *Telling the Truth: Preaching about Sexual and Domestic Violence*, eds. John S. McClure and Nancy J. Ramsay (Cleveland, OH: United Church Press, 1998), 53, 56.

4. Robert J. Schreiter, C.P.P.S. *The Ministry of Reconciliation: Spirituality and Strategies* (Maryknoll, NY: Orbis, 1998), 59, 66.

5. Ibid., chapter 5.

6. Desmond Tutu and Mpho Tutu, *The Book of Forgiving* (New York: HarperOne, 2014), 148, 155.

7. Ibid., 154.

8. For a remarkable story of unlikely relationships being renewed, see "Portraits of Reconciliation" from *New York Times Magazine*, April 2014, available at: http://invisiblechildren.com/blog/2014/04/07/ny-times-magazine-portraits-reconciliation/.

9. Lk 23:34; Acts 7:60.

10. Tutu and Tutu, *Book of Forgiving*, 9.

11. The Tutus' book includes a series of very concrete exercises. Also recommended: www.loveandforgive.org, www.theforgiveness-project.com, and www.forgivenessfoundation.org.

12. Tutu and Tutu, *Book of Forgiving* 26.

13. Corrie ten Boom with J. and S. Sherril, *The Hiding Place* (New York: Bantam, 1971), 217.

14. Corrie ten Boom, "I'm Still Learning to Forgive," *Guideposts Magazine* (1972).

15. Ibid.

16. Craig Bryan Larson, ed., 750 *Engaging Illustrations for Preachers, Teachers, and Writers* (Grand Rapids, MI: Baker Books, 2007), 180.

9. Repent

1. Marie M. Fortune, "Preaching Forgiveness?" in *Telling the Truth*, eds. John S. McClure and Nancy J. Ramsay (Cleveland: United Church Press, 1998), 56.

2. Charles Williams, *The Forgiveness of Sin*.

3. Tutu and Tutu, *Book of Forgiving*, 177.

4. See "The Michigan Model: Medical Malpractice and Patient Safety," accessed at http://www.uofmhealth.org/michigan-model-medical-malpractice-and-patient-safety-umhs.

5. La Rochefoucauld, *The Moral Maxims and Reflections of the Duke De La Rochefoucauld: With an Introduction and Notes* (London: Forgotten Books, 2015).

6. Tutu and Tutu, *Book of Forgiving*, 178.

7. Ibid., 185.

8. Ibid., 186.

9. J. Green quoted in McMillen, *Currents of Malice* (Portsmouth, NH: Peter Randall, 1980).

10. Ibid.

11. Charles W. Upham, *Salem Witchcraft II* (Mineola, NY: Dover Publications, 2010), 509–510.

10. Problem Solve

1. The language of "hard," "soft" (aka "positional"), and "principled" bargaining is used in Roger Fisher and William Ury, with Bruce Patton, *Getting to Yes: Negotiating Agreement Without Giving In*, 2nd ed. (New York: Penguin, 1991), see especially chapter 1.

2. Fisher and Ury, *Getting to Yes*, 2nd ed. (New York: Penguin, 1991), 158.

3. Ibid., 21.

4. Ibid., 40.

5. Ibid., 42.

6. Ibid., 56.

7. Ibid., 60.

8. Bishop Joseph Hall of Norwich, *Hard Measure* (1647) quoted in *The Organ, Its History and Construction* by Edward Hopkins, 71.

11. Be Trustworthy, Not Necessarily Trusting

1. Fisher and Ury, *Getting to Yes*, 159.

2. Ibid., 81.

3. Aquinas, *Summa Theologiae* II–II.58.1, vol. 3, 1428–1429.

4. Fisher and Ury devote all of chapter 5 in *Getting to Yes* to this topic.

5. Jn 20:24–29.

6. Mother Teresa, *One Heart Full of Love* (Cincinnati, OH: St. Anthony Messenger Press, 1988), 119.

7. Fisher and Ury, *Getting to Yes*, 142–143.

8. Howard Raiffa, *The Art and Science of Negotiations* (Cambridge, MA: Harvard UP, 1982).

9. Fisher and Ury, *Getting to Yes*, 97–106.

10. "To The Very Reverend A. Martin" written July 3, 1846, in *Journals and Letters of Mother Theodore Guerin*, Part V, "A Record of Difficulties"—edited with notes by Sr. Mary Theodosia Mug (St. Mary-of-the-Woods, 1937).

11. Quoted in Herman J. Alerding, *The Diocese of Vincennes* (Indianapolis, 1874), 74, 177–178, which includes the text of Fr. Ernest Audran's eulogy.

12. "To the Right Reverend Cel. De la Hailandière Bishop of Vincennes," written March 8, 1846, in *Journals and Letters of Mother Theodore Guerin*, Part V, "A Record of Difficulties," edited with notes by Sr. Mary Theodosia Mug (St. Mary-of-the-Woods, IN: St. Mary-of-the-Woods, 1937).

13. Joseph M. White, "Path to Sainthood and Episcopal Leadership," *U. S. Catholic Historian* 29, no. 1 (Winter 2011): 73–94.

12. Practice Prudence

1. Lewis Carroll, *Alice's Adventures in Wonderland* (Boston: Lathrop Publishing Co., 1898), 53.

2. Stone, Patton, and Heen refer to this as the Third Story to contrast it with My Story or Your Story. See Stone, Patton, and Heen, *Difficult Conversations*, 149ff.

3. Sarah Harris, quoted in Prudence Crandall, "Letter to the *Windham County Advertiser* (May 7, 1833)," published in *Fruits of Colonization*, 1833.

4. Samuel J. May, *Some Recollections of Our Antislavery Conflict* (Boston: Fields, Osgood, and Co., 1869), 39–72.

5. Ibid.

6. Prudence Crandall, "Letter to Simeon Jocelyn (April 17, 1833)," published in "Abolition Letters Collected by Captain Arthur B. Spingarn," *Journal of Negro History*, vol. XVIII, 1933, 82–84.

For a further dive into the work of the Harvard Negotiation Project, see:

Douglas Stone, Bruce Patton, and Sheila Heen. *Difficult Conversations: How to Discuss What Matters Most*, 10th Anniversary Edition. New York: Penguin Books, 2010.

Douglas Stone and Sheila Heen. *Thanks for the Feedback: The Science and Art of Receiving Feedback Well Even When It Is Off Base, Unfair, Poorly Delivered, and Frankly, You're Not in the Mood*. New York: Penguin Books, 2014.

Roger Fisher and William Ury with Bruce Patton. *Getting to Yes*. New York: Penguin Books, 1981.

Roger Fisher and Alan Sharp. *Getting It Done: How to Lead When You're Not in Charge*. New York: Harper Collins, 1998.

Roger Fisher and Daniel L. Shapiro. *Beyond Reason: Using Emotions as You Negotiate*. New York: Penguin Books, 2005.

Ann M. Garrido is associate professor of homiletics at Aquinas Institute of Theology in St. Louis, Missouri. While her first passion is teaching, for more than fifteen years she has found herself increasingly drawn to administrative roles. Garrido has served as senior editor of *Human Development Magazine* and is the author of five books, including the award-winning *Redeeming Administration*. She travels nationally and internationally doing conflict education and mediation work in both the business and church worlds.

Also *by*
Ann M. Garrido

Find Comfort and Grace in Your Vocation

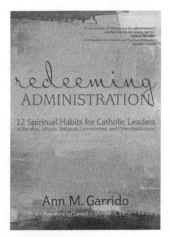

Redeeming Administration offers twelve spiritual habits—each illuminated through the story of a Catholic saint—that show administrators how to experience their work as a crucial ministry of the Church. Ann M. Garrido continues to provide keen insight and thoughtful dialogue to readers in need of lifted spirits.
224 pages, $14.95

Available wherever books and eBooks are sold.

For more information, visit **avemariapress.com.**

Additional Resources are available as **FREE** downloadable **PDFs** at **www.avemariapress.com.**

AVE MARIA PRESS
A Ministry of the United States
Province of Holy Cross